TWELVE YEARS OF DELUSIONS

MEMORIES OF MY TWELVE-YEAR STRUGGLE WITH BIPOLAR DISORDER

Wolf Blaser Jr.

Archway Publishing books may be ordered through booksellers or by contacting:

Archway Publishing
1663 Liberty Drive
Bloomington, IN 47403
www.archwaypublishing.com
1 (888) 242-5904

ISBN: 978-1-4808-6838-0 (sc)
ISBN: 978-1-4808-6837-3 (e)

Library of Congress Control Number: 2018958124

Print information available on the last page.

Archway Publishing rev. date: 9/18/2018

CONTENTS

CHAPTER 1

GROWING UP

My name is Wolf Blaser Jr. I was born in Topeka, Kansas, on November 27, 1968. I have mostly lived in Topeka for the past forty-eight years. I attended Bishop Elementary School and then went on to Jardine Middle School and graduated from Topeka West High School in 1987. I grew up across the street from Bishop Elementary School; my parents moved in 1987. My father worked for a local construction company during the '70s and then started his own construction company in the early '80s. He was president of his company until he retired in 2010.

My mother was a stay-at-home mom to my sister and me when we were babies. After graduating from high school, she earned a business degree from Washburn University and worked as a Realtor for several years. She then became a secretary at my father's construction company and worked there for many years. Despite working full-time, my mother would always find the time to take me to Cub Scouts when I was in elementary school.

I have one sister, and she is two years older than me. She attended the same elementary, middle, and high schools as I did, and like my mother, she graduated from Washburn University with a degree in business. She went on to work at my father's construction company and would later resign to earn a nursing degree from Washburn University.

Living across the street from Bishop Elementary School made it easy to get to school, and Jardine Middle School was about one mile from my house. I recall struggling the first few years of elementary school; the feelings I had when starting kindergarten were similar to the feelings I had years later. I don't remember much of elementary school, but I do remember crying in third grade while working on an assignment. I don't have a specific memory of this, but I vaguely remember being forced to write with my right hand despite being left-handed.

Having said that, I don't believe anything was a trigger for my future mental illness. I had several friends—some older than me—who lived in the neighborhood. I would spend a lot of time after school with them. We went to the playground at school or played hide-and-seek in the alleys behind houses. We used to have snowball fights during the winter, and I would dig igloos out of the piles of snow on the driveway.

When I was around ten years old, I began to play baseball and basketball. Later, I started shooting competitive rifles for several years. I received the distinguished expert medal for marksmanship and was a Kansas state champion. I shot at the nationals in Camp Perry, Ohio, a couple of times. After shooting, I started to play football for the first time in middle school.

In 1982, when I was thirteen years old, I started chewing tobacco. A friend introduced me to it, and I have been hooked ever since. The buzz felt so good, and it is the reason I continue to chew tobacco to this day thirty-five years later.

I recall feeling a lot more tired than usual when I was in middle school. The chewing tobacco started to negatively affect my state of mind. Because I could not chew tobacco during school, I began to develop withdrawal symptoms, which resulted in chronic fatigue.

In high school, I lettered in football, basketball, and track and field. When I played football, I was all-state my senior year and all-city for two years. In basketball, I received the player-of-the-week honor in the *Topeka Capital Journal* but did not make all-city. During high school, I was an average student and never took honors classes. In my senior year, my girlfriend and I were voted homecoming king and queen. I spent most of my senior year with my girlfriend and my friends.

I started college on a football scholarship at the University of Kansas. I was also recruited by other schools, such as Oklahoma and Colorado, but I decided to stay close to Topeka. I quickly found out that I should have worked harder in high school. My first semester at KU was tough. Balancing football and school required discipline, which I lacked. Football usually went from noon until five in the evening, so I would take classes in the morning and would study after practice. In my first semester at KU, I received a very low GPA. To be eligible to play football, students were required to maintain twelve credit hours or more. I had a chemistry class that was worth five credit hours, and I had sixteen credit hours in total. If I failed my chemistry class, I would have only eleven credit hours in total, making me ineligible to continue playing football.

In the middle of the semester, I knew I was failing the class, but I could not drop it, because I was playing special teams on the football team. In addition, there was a coaching change during my freshman and sophomore years at KU. As a result, I stopped playing football at the university the summer after my first year, but I continued to study at KU for another year in hopes of getter better grades. In the end, I decided a smaller-class setting was what I needed to make it through university.

Therefore, I transferred to Washburn University and took the core classes needed for engineering, including math and science. My goal was to get a degree in civil engineering, so I spent a lot of time studying at the library with my classmates. During my time at Washburn, I met my future wife. She was attending Washburn at the same time as I was and was completing her undergraduate degree.

After spending a couple of years at Washburn and completing the required undergraduate classes, I transferred to Kansas State University. At Kansas State University, I lived in an apartment complex with a roommate from Washburn. It was a fifteen-minute drive to campus from the apartment, so I ended up spending a lot of time studying on campus. I completed the remainder of the requirements for a degree in civil engineering and graduated in 1993.

I proposed to the woman I'd met at Washburn in Manhattan my senior year, and we married in September 1993. We lived together in an apartment complex in Topeka; she was working at the hospital, and I was starting my career. We eventually moved into a home in 1996 so we could start a family.

Throughout these years, I did not have a sense that anything was wrong with me mentally. I had my up days and down days just like everyone else, but I did not have any thought disorders or visions. Upon graduating with a degree in engineering, I was hired by my father's construction company. This was the early '90s. I purchased a briefcase and started as a junior estimator. I never interviewed with other companies.

Since my father's company was a construction business that primarily specialized in the industrial sector and not an engineering business, structural concrete design and other subjects did not apply to my new position of estimator; nor did my education overall. The drawings and calculations were already completed by the time I started working on them, and the projects were small, consisting of installing doors and replacing concrete floors.

I discovered that the on-the-job learning started on the first day. At the time, estimators would perform their tasks by hand, using a pencil and paper, but I had a calculator to do the math. I was very driven and believed that someday the company would grow, so I always looked at the large projects up for bid around the city. But deep down, I knew they were out of reach.

I took on all the small jobs at the company and believed I had to start small and learn the ropes before I could take on much larger projects. As an estimator, I learned about the minor details of every job. When a job was completed, I would analyze the bid price and determine whether money had been made. I benefited because the company performed tasks on a time and material basis. This meant I had to keep track of the labor, equipment, material, and subcontractors per job and bill the owner with a markup. If a project changed in scope or ran over cost, a change order was issued to cover the additional work.

Gradually, the size of the work increased, and by using prior costs, I could create a cost structure for certain jobs. When a potential client asked about cost, I could generally give the client a ballpark cost estimate on the spot. This was crucial because clients often wanted to know the costs right away. Over the years, I worked on many different projects and gained knowledge of not only the costs but also the implementation of the work. I learned a great deal from the people I worked with, and there was always something new to learn in the construction field—things such as which tools to use and what methods to apply.

Gradually, I moved into a position of project manager, while keeping my estimating duties. My role as project manager involved scheduling the materials and subcontractors and working with other project managers in coordinating the manpower needed to complete the work. I always loved work that involved water and wastewater treatment, whether it be adding a new pump station or a new addition to a plant. I had a genuine love of water—both sewer and drinking water. To me, the sound of water as it made its way through a treatment plant was reminiscent of a waterfall or the ocean.

My first opportunity to work on a wastewater plant came in the mid-’90s. The job was large enough to bid on but not so large that bidding would not be possible for us. After the estimation and bidding, we came in second. The first-place bid was around 10 percent lower than my bid. In the construction industry, when bids are made on jobs that are public, such as a wastewater plant for a city, the bidder must provide a bid bond. With a bid bond, 5 percent of the bid is turned in to ensure security in case the bid comes in too low. In the '70s and '80s, the bid bond was used if the bidder decided not to go ahead with the job because the bid was too low. The bid bond acted as an insurance policy. In the '90s and thereafter, the bid bond could not be forfeited if the bidder decided to pull out of the bid because of a mathematical error. In this case, the low bidder decided not to perform the work because of a math error, and my bid was used by the city. This was the first water or wastewater job that I was awarded. The project lasted about a year, and I started to target these kinds of jobs more thereafter.

Several water treatment jobs were awarded to us, including modification to an existing water plant and two new water pump stations. Aside from the wastewater plant job, these projects were worth less than $1 million. At the time, we could obtain bonds without extra financial involvement. We would perform and complete the jobs, and the company would receive a profit for each job.

My next break involved working on a wastewater pump station and completing the piping work associated with it. When I placed my bid, the bid came in over $5 million. I saw this opportunity as a step up for the company—something that could lead to possibly larger projects in the future.

I struggled with this project in early 2000. At the time, I had a two-year-old son and an infant daughter. Like every parent, I was juggling work and family. My wife also worked during this time, so if a child was sick, one of us needed to stay home. The project lasted about one and a half years, and during this time, I wanted to increase the number of the jobs if an opportunity presented itself.

By this time it was close to 2002, and a large addition to a wastewater plant for the city of Topeka was up for bidding. We ended up being the low bidder on the project, but the bids were relatively close to each other. The project was roughly three times the size of the pump station job. Based on the size, the company needed to acquire larger equipment and ramp up the labor force. During this bid, I discovered there were more phases of work to bid on at the plant that would span the course of many years.

replaced. I told her that I would take care of the tires for her. On July 4, we drove in my vehicle to pick up her car, and she drove to the tire store with her vehicle while I followed her. The tires on her vehicle were then replaced, and I paid for them like I'd said I would. This process lasted until midafternoon. However, my wife and I were having friends over to celebrate Independence Day, and I needed to be home for that. When I got home, I told my wife what I had done for the lady, and she told me that I should not have done that. I, on the other hand, thought it was a nice thing to do, helping someone else out. However, given it all started in group therapy for mental health patients, it was not appropriate. The Independence Day evening went on without much excitement for me. Everyone else enjoyed a great evening, but I just felt numb. On the following week, my wife informed the Stormont Vail staff of what I had done for the lady, and they set up an arrangement with her, wherein I would be reimbursed over several months.

During my time at the facility and group therapy, I was not working. There was comfort in knowing that my job was, nevertheless, secure despite what was happening to me at the time. Unfortunately, for others with mental illness, such job security could be elusive; many end up losing their jobs and access to the best mental health medications.

For the remainder of 2005, I did not experience any visions while falling asleep at night or when trying to nap during the day. I still had depression but did the best I could to help around the house and take care of my two children. By then, my son was seven years old, and my daughter was four. I performed the tasks that most fathers would do for their children, such as giving my daughter her baths at night and helping my son with school-related things.

I would check the bathwater several times when giving my daughter a bath, to make sure the water was not too hot. Unlike with most parents, this simple task turned into an obsessive compulsion disorder for me. It could be anything, from checking the bathwater to making sure the stove was turned off or the doors are locked in the house. The disorder can control a person's entire thought process when triggered.

My wife would assign tasks as simple as taking the trash out or loading and unloading the dishwasher, to involve me as much as possible. Again, most people do these sorts of tasks all the time, but with the bipolar disorder, the tasks took on a new meaning to me; at the time, it was an accomplishment for me to perform these simple tasks successfully.

In summer 2005, I developed the first of a few amazing abilities that I thought I had. This one involved controlling the weather, specifically, the clouds in the sky. If I stared at them, it was my belief that I could stop them from moving. This period of concentration only lasted between five to ten seconds maximum, but it started to work in my mind, and I thought I really had this amazing ability. In some cases, the clouds would stop, and the wind would die down. Then, after I stared at them, they would move again, and the wind would pick up with a gust, as though it had stopped for a brief period of time. I tried not to share this information with others. I confided in my wife about many things, but I knew she would think this was crazy. If I started talking to strangers about things like my ability to immobilize clouds, they would certainly get the impression that I had lost my mind.

From that point onward, my episodes of staring at the clouds increased. I probably looked at clouds two or three times a week. By that point, I had confided this to my wife, but I would sneak out to the back side of the house or make sure she was not around before I started looking at clouds. She would have known what I was doing and would have been upset with me.

I would stop the clouds during the day and again later in the evening. I would then watch the local weather forecast to see if anything unusual was mentioned regarding the clouds or the weather. In my mind, I was looking for anything—one word or facial expression—that would confirm my delusions. Something as simple as the forecaster saying that the wind had really picked up during the afternoon would put my mind back into hypomania mode. Fortunately, there was never anything that could have set me into full-blown mania again, such as a comment made by the meteorologist regarding the clouds having stopped this afternoon for a brief period. In my mind, I thought controlling the clouds might have something to do with what I had seen during the night of June 11, when I saw blue skies with clouds. Could this mean that I was, in fact, in control of them? Similar questions were constantly going on in my head. Yet, this was only the tip of the iceberg—the magnitude and scope of my amazing abilities would grow.

At the beginning of fall 2005, I watched a movie on the television set in our main bedroom. At the end of the commercials, a man and woman would briefly discuss the movie before it resumed. Toward the end of the movie, there were parts out of there and was one of the largest employers in the city along with Boeing, and because one of the founders of Microsoft owned the Seattle Seahawks, I wondered whether my grandparents had a connection to Microsoft as well.

Companies in Topeka that I thought had connections to my grandparents included Capitol Federal Bank. I started to believe my grandparents had a substantial amount of money with the bank. The bank's motto mentions the color blue, and I believed my grandparents were associated with the bank because my parents, sister, grandmother, and I had blue eyes. I tried to work this eye color into my delusional thinking. There was obviously nothing that could be proved.

There were several shopping areas in Topeka that I thought my grandparents were involved in, such as developments along Wanamaker in the 1980s. When my father started his company, one of the first jobs he completed was building a large stormwater collection system under the parking lot at the Plaza West development. I believed my grandparents financed the shopping area and let my father construct the collection box. I never asked my father if this was true, but it is unlikely.

At first, Commerce Bank & Trust was located in the Holiday shopping area, and later it expanded into a building close to the McDonald's my grandfather operated. My relatives knew the owners and had done business with the bank, which further added to my delusions in thinking my grandparents owned shares in it. My grandparents banked there while they owned the McDonald's franchises, and I had banked there since the early '80s, starting with only a savings account. To me, this was all somehow connected.

Every new bit of information that came my way kept me preoccupied for weeks. Once, I found a picture of an auto parts store in a book about Topeka. The store was called Lacy Auto Parts and was located across the street from the downtown McDonald's my grandparents operated, where Azura bank is now located. This was significant to me because my grandparents' last name was Lacy.

When my grandfather passed away in 1998, I was given a fishing tackle box that contained small tools, screws, and bolts. Inside the tackle box was a matchbox with Commerce Bank's name on it. Two of the bank's branches were listed on the inside, and the box contained a pencil from a large insurance company based in Topeka, which is now owned by Guggenheim, as well as a crayon from the American Crayon Company. On top of it all, the tackle box had "Plano" written on its side. Plano, Texas, is outside of Dallas, and Frito-Lay's corporate headquarters are based in

Plano. Coincidentally, there is a Frito-Lay manufacturing plant located in Topeka, which made me believe my grandfather had stocks in Frito-Lay.

I thought many companies had some connection to my grandparents, but there was only one major company I believed I had some involvement with.

Facebook was started in early 2004, but I believed I was involved in its creation. It wasn't until later that I tried to piece together my involvement in the creation of Facebook. I was picked to be social chairman of the local chapter of the Active 20-30 Club. Serving in this capacity required notifying all active members, as well as members that had aged out of the club, of upcoming events. I was never was any good at working with computers. I was able to send emails and do the basics with Microsoft Office, but what I had the most trouble with was notifying the members of the club's upcoming events. At the time, there were lists of members and email addresses, but there was no way of sending out multiple emails at once. I ended up typing the members' emails into a separate file in Microsoft Outlook, and I would then click on everyone's email and send the message that way. This system was flawed from the beginning—some members were never informed—but it was the best I could do considering my computer skills.

Since I was having problems contacting members, I thought there must be a better way to perform this task—Facebook. There is absolutely nothing true about my involvement with Facebook. My involvement was a complete fabrication and delusion.

Later in my life, I would begin to laugh at this delusion. I don't have a Facebook account; nor am I a social person, because of my mental illness. Wouldn't you think I would have an account if I had been involved in the creation of the platform?

Over the years, my delusions continued. I do not know much about my grandfather from Germany. What I do know is that he was a soldier in World War II, he died during the war, and he is buried in Holland with many other soldiers.

My grandfather died from complications after being shot in the leg during World War II. I never thought much about him until I saw a picture of him in uniform with a moustache in my father's office at his house. Later into my years of mental illness, I would concentrate on what rank my grandfather had held during the war. His uniform lapels had three eagles on both sides. I asked my father about his father's rank, but he did not know.

When my sister came back from a trip to Germany, it got me thinking even more about this. On her trip, my uncle had given her several pictures of my grandfather when he was young, including pictures of his time in the military. Thumbing through the pictures got my mind racing. One picture in particular caught my eye. It was a picture of him with a group of other German soldiers. There were two soldiers on the ground with their legs out in front, and the remaining soldiers were in a row behind them. I started to wonder if he was part of some secret experiment during World War II.

My grandfather from the United States was just as intriguing as my grandmother, but my parents did not talk much about him either. He had grown up poor in the hills of Kentucky and hunted animals for food. He later moved to Chicago and worked at a bank and then met my grandmother in Chicago and married her. They both reached their fifty-year wedding anniversary.

One of my most significant delusions involved my grandparents and their last name—Lacy. All it took was a trip to the funeral home, which I did a couple of times a year to place flowers on my mom and grandparents' graves. My mom was buried outside, but my grandparents' crypt was inside the mausoleum. As I stood there for a moment, another couple entered and looked at the names on the wall. I overheard one of them say to the other that she wanted to see Rockefellers' grave. I didn't know what she was talking about, but as I walked back to my truck, I started to think that maybe my grandfather was related to the Rockefellers. There was the famous John Rockefeller with Standard Oil, and he had a brother named Frank. My grandfather's first name was Frank, and I began to wonder if my grandfather was Frank Rockefeller.

Then I started to think about my grandmother and who she might have been. I became confused and randomly settled on the name Vanderbilt. By coincidence, the original building in the Holiday shopping mall that housed the first Commerce Bank was now a western clothing store called Vanderbilt's. Could there be a connection between two of the richest families in the early twentieth century? I tried to not think about this further, as my mind had all the information it needed to keep the thoughts and delusions going.

CHAPTER 4

PLAYING THE RADIO GAME

Most of us listen to the radio from time to time. It helps calm anxiety in any given situation. Most of us also know the lyrics to our favorite songs, and some melodies are embedded in our minds long after we hear them. With my mental illness, songs turned into weapons, and a battle started in my mind that lasted twelve years.

Hundreds of songs are created each year, and multiple radio stations, as well as satellite radio, are available to us to listen to. I listen to both local radio stations and satellite radio and like to hum the tunes of each song. In my situation, the songs came from the thoughts I was having at the time—it was what I believed in my mental state. For example, in the past, traveling to Kansas City with the kids or by myself would only further fuel my delusions. I would always hear the same song before or after going through the tollbooth on the highway. It was probably a coincidence, but from my perspective, the radio stations were reading my mind and anticipating my next move.

With radio, I believed the stations were trying to program songs in sequence with my thoughts—whether they be about my wife, kids, work, or my years in high school. If I was thinking about my wife, a song from the '90s would play. Similarly, when I thought about my high school girlfriend, songs from the '80s would play. If I thought about elementary or middle school, a '70s song would come on. I can't recall if I had a crush on someone back in my elementary and middle school days that would explain the songs.

During this time, songs inflicted maximum damage to my mind and my thought disorders. I believed the songs themselves were specifically targeted to affect my state of mind.

Years later, I made a smart move and would only play classic rock stations to prevent this from happening. To this day, I primarily listen to Sirius XM channel 25 in the car and 99.3 the Eagle and 101 the Fox around the house. I refuse to listen to songs from the 2000s.

Listening to music or the radio was unavoidable in certain stores or restaurants, as they would have music playing constantly. These times did not provide reprieve. Over the years, I learned to tune the music out.

There were some instances when it felt like either I was catching up to the music or the music was catching up to me. For instance, I would walk into a store that was not playing music, and minutes later the music would start to play. In these situations, my thoughts would not stop until a new thought disorder emerged. I would get confused and wonder why I had not heard the music as I walked into the store or wonder if I was perhaps deaf. I wondered if the music had started playing just to mess with my mind. Most of the main radio stations would play songs from the '70s or '80s. I would sometimes try to sing along but many times did not know the lyrics, or I could not hear the songs properly. Depending on the song, the situation, or the state of my mind, I believed the songs tried to confuse me and tried to spark my hypomania.

Unlike satellite radio, local music stations have commercials in between songs. Most of the commercials are local, but again, this proved to be torturous. As I listened to them, I would pick up information that would elevate my mind. The more my mind was elevated, the more my thought disorders occurred. I can still hear the words to songs and think back to the struggles I had with music, but I have broken through that barrier. I no longer control the songs in my head, and the songs no longer control me.

During summer 2006, the family took a vacation to Disneyland and San Diego. I did not have a good time during the trip but tried to do my best. I have a picture of us at Disneyland, and you would never know I was struggling with mental illness. Our time at Disneyland was uneventful compared to the visions I was having or the voices I was hearing. My first vision happened after we rented a car, drove to San Diego, and checked in at the hotel. We rented a cottage-type room in San Diego within the inner bay area. Every guest had a cottage near the beach, but the beach was not a part of the Pacific Ocean. There was a pool on the grounds of the hotel, but no restaurants.

We drove to the local grocery store and bought food to cook in the cottage. For some reason, I felt people were looking at me while we strolled down the aisles. When we paid for the groceries and started putting them in the car, I noticed a couple of people standing nearby. With my back turned to them, I remember hearing one of them say it looked like a storm was coming in. I had noticed some storm clouds earlier, and given my state of mind and the belief that I could control the clouds and weather, I believed they heard what I was thinking and thought they had made that comment to try to elevate my mental state. I spent the rest of the afternoon and evening thinking about what they had said.

One night on our vacation, we spent some time at the beach. I remember sitting there and looking up at the clouds—my mind consumed with thoughts of the weather—while the kids were having fun. I have a picture of my two children from that day, but instead of thinking about the fun they were having picking up seashells, I think about how zoned out I was on that beach and how I missed the chance to spend time with them when they were young.

There were many other times over the years where I felt like I missed the opportunity to spend time with them. We don't realize how fast time goes and how quickly kids grow up and become more independent. My kids are at the age now where they don't want to spend a lot of time with me.

One night at the cottage, I had visions. While trying to fall asleep, I started to have visions of people's heads. They would pop up in front of me and then disappear to the back left-hand side. Over the years, this would happen often. The interesting thing about these visions was that some of the heads would start to scream. I could not hear the screaming, but I could make out their expressions. I believed they were screaming because they were going someplace they did not want to go. At the cottage, I saw these visions two nights in a row but did not recognize any of the people. I think they were just random people.

We spent another day at the resort lounging by the swimming pool. While I was lying on a chair getting some sun with my sunglasses on, I noticed a man and woman speaking German—I assumed they were vacationing from Germany—and the strangest thing happened. As I looked at the man, he said something to his wife, who immediately turned around and looked at me. He said something in German that I could not understand, and my mind started spinning. What did he say? Did he say the word "witch" in German? I had taken a couple of German classes in high school and had traveled to Germany several times over the years to see relatives, but I could not translate what he was saying. I took this and thought about it for months. It felt like I was creating a library of thoughts in my head, and the thoughts just kept popping up, driving me crazy.

While in San Diego, the family took a trip to both a safari park and Legoland. The weather during our trip to the safari park was hot with high humidity. The reason I remember the weather is because I ended up carrying the children all around the park. Whenever we came across a water fountain, we all had to fill up.

The trip to Legoland was not as hot and humid as the trip to the safari park. We toured Legoland and saw the amazing Lego structures. With both parks, there were plenty of tourists around, and my mind would race, wondering what people were saying and whether it was something I was thinking. The trip back to Topeka through Kansas City took a complete day with a layover in Phoenix. When we arrived in Kansas City, I finally got some relief. The drive from Kansas City was mainly quiet, with my wife and kids asleep in the car for the entire drive. We arrived in Topeka, and everyone quickly went to sleep, leaving the suitcases for the next day.

CHAPTER 5

PLAYING THE MEDIA GAME

Not only did I play a game with the radio, I also played a game with the television programming and movies. With television, it moved along with my thoughts; for instance, when I thought of something in my mind, the actor or actress on television would say or do what I was thinking. It got so bad sometimes that I would just shut the television off and stop watching, regardless of what show was playing. I believed my thoughts were being manipulated and acted out on the television. Sometimes, I would change the station to a movie channel, like HBO or Starz, so I would not have to put up with the commercials. I believed there was some type of connection between my eyes and ears and the television. The same thing would happen with movies as well. In my mind, it felt as though I was playing an interactive game with the television that flowed with my thoughts and never stopped creating more delusions and thought disorders.

When the nightly national news came on at 5:30 p.m., the stories being reported matched with what I had read during the day in the paper or had seen online on my computer or phone. It makes sense that any major story that I'd read during the day would be reported in the national news later that same evening. I thought of things differently in my mind; I believed that some of the news was created in my head.

The commercials were just as effective in my mind, like the radio stations I listened to. Certain commercials would come on at times when my mind was in hypomania. A Capital One commercial or an Arby's commercial would pop up on the television at just the right time. Commercials for drugs would always come on during the nightly news. I would watch *The Today Show* in the mornings before work and think I was controlling the programming of the show.

As for the weather channel, I believed I was in control of it and that the meteorologists only knew the upcoming forecast because I was feeding it to them. I would also look for a deeper and special meaning in the temperatures during the forecasts, especially if the temperature was going to be 87 or 77 or 66.

In the final years of my struggle, I was better mentally and would choose specific channels to watch and stay away from others that I knew would affect my mind. When a commercial that had affected me in the past would come on, I would immediately switch the channel.

Print media, such as the local newspaper, was similar, in that it could elevate my mind, but not as dramatically as did television. Every morning, I would read the local newspaper, starting with the front page and working my way through every page. Every time I would turn the page, I wondered what would show up on the next. Again, depending on what I read on the prior page, in my mind, I thought I could predict what was on the next page, even though there is no way that I could change the printed words on the paper as I read. My thought disorders about the paper only added to my mental illness.

I also spent a lot of time trying to piece together anything that had to do with the titles of a story. It was of special significance to me if the titles had any numbers associated with it. I would also try to piece a word from one story together with another word from another story in the paper. For instance, if one story had the word "accident" and another from a different page had the words "truck tips over on its side," I would associate them. Word association was something I would do for many years.

Print magazines or books were not any different either. Over the years, I had the habit of going to Barnes & Noble in Topeka to pick up magazines. I started to believe that when I walked up to the magazine section to look for a specific magazine, the cover page and text would transform into whatever I might have been thinking about. I liked picking up the latest issue of *Fortune* or *Forbes* magazine, as they would always feature a company or topic that I had been be thinking about, such as Facebook or Microsoft, or run an article on one of those companies. I always would buy the Fortune 500 issue of *Fortune*, which ranked the richest people and the largest companies in America. I would go through both lists and locate the mentioned individuals and their related companies and let my mind work through the different scenarios or ways in which I was involved with them.

Books had the same effect on me as magazines. I had purchased a book on the history of Topeka that contained photographs dated as far back as the late 1800s. I would look at a certain picture and look for anything that would enable my delusional mind. For example, there was a picture from the 1950s of a man riding his horse up to the bank teller of a Capitol Federal Bank branch. I was only interested in a specific part of the picture—the teller's window had a sign stating the bank had $200 million in deposits. There was another picture of this bank that piqued my interest; it featured a group of men standing next to a truck crane marked "MW Watson," which was the company my father had started to work for some time after I was born. I tried hard to see if I could spot my grandfather in the picture, but I could not find him.

I was not an avid reader as a child. It took me several tries to read a sentence, as my mind would change the actual words in the book with other words. It was almost as though I was slightly dyslexic. Spelling and English were not my strong points in school, and I briefly thought this handicap I had with reading might have had something to do with my delusions related to print media.

CHAPTER 6

COLORS AND WHAT THEY MEAN TO ME

Though there are many different colors, my obsession was solely on the five colors of the Olympic rings—blue, yellow, black, green, and red. For me, these colors represented the balance of our planet. For example, I would associate blue with the color of the sky and of the ocean, yellow with the color of the sun, black with the darkness, green with the color of the grass and trees, and red with the color of the core of the earth. If one or more colors were missing in this balance, what kind of impact would this have on our planet?

Some might consider the way I interpreted colors as crazy. In my mind, a color could represent a person. The Olympics originated in Greece many thousands of years ago. Was it possible that each color represented a Greek god at the time? I associated blue with Poseidon, as he was the god of the seas in Greek mythology. As for Hades, I associated him with red because he was from the underworld. However, I could not associate Zeus with any color.

I found the word "Hades" to be interesting, as it had the word "Des" in it, which my mind related to my grandmother and the city of Des Moines. My mind added this city to my long list of disorders and went over it repeatedly.

I had taken a trip to Los Angeles with my relatives in the summer of 1984 to watch the Olympics. As my aunt and uncle owned a franchise of McDonald's, they were able to procure tickets to the games. I had a fun vacation and we saw several Olympic events. This was my first time visiting Los Angeles, so we did the things tourist do—bodysurfing in the ocean, walking along Rodeo Drive, and eating at nice restaurants. At the time, I was a freshman at Topeka West High School and had retired from competing at rifle competitions.

Prior to my mental illness, I had never thought much about that trip to Los Angeles or about the Olympics. The first connection I tried to make in my mind was McDonald's and their sponsorship of the Olympics. I looked up who had won the Gold medal in 1984 in shooting in prone position. In my mind, I thought I was somehow at the Olympics in Los Angeles, shooting for a medal. The plausibility of that happening was as delusional as the thought itself, yet it did not matter in my mind; only the thoughts of winning the gold medal in shooting did.

I want to discuss my delusion regarding the color red. On a sunny day, I would sit outside and close my eyes. My vision would turn completely red. This was simply due to the sunlight making its way through my eyelids, which then caused my vision to turn red. However, in my state of mind, I believed that the red I was seeing was something coming from within. I thought that it was strong enough in power to hold the sun at a precise distance from the earth; if it were any closer, it would get hotter; any farther, and it would only get colder. When I shut my eyes and saw red, it felt like the sun was getting closer. My body would then warm up when this took place, which only further enabled my delusion.

Several times over the years when I would close my eyes, I would see a green or purple haze. At first, I only saw the purple clouds circling around, but later, the green clouds would start to appear. When both clouds were in my vision, it seemed like a battle was taking place between them. First, the purple cloud would appear, and then a green cloud would push the purple one away until it disappeared. Sometimes I would even see people in the clouds, like ghosts. I didn't know whether the clouds had any significance in relation to anything that was going on with me at that time. I started to associate the purple clouds with Willie Wonka because he wore a purple suit, and I would associate the green clouds with Saint John the Baptist because the trim and roof of the Baptist church down the road from my house was green. I had to find some association.

Only two specific visions included these colors. One vision had a person sitting on a throne with two cats in front. These cats had teeth like saber-toothed tigers, and they were larger than house cats but smaller than tigers. When I would see this man in a vision, a green haze would erase him from top to bottom. I wondered whether the green color I was seeing somehow represented saints that removed him from his throne. Was this person a king from many years ago? The second vision was of a man with purple pants walking toward me when my eyes were closed.

My mind would also try to manipulate the colors of the traffic lights. I thought that I could somehow control them by looking at them. There were many times over the years when I would be stopped at a light, and I would look at it, and it would turn green. Just as I believed I could change the words of newspapers and magazines, I believed I had the power to change the traffic lights. Of course, it was only coincidence that the signal would turn green when I looked at it. Some of the lights in Topeka are still controlled by timers, but many are now monitored by a camera system that determines the traffic load in the lanes. My mind would try to push itself to a hypomania mode every time I encountered a light, so that I could think I was fully in control of them, regardless of the light. Eventually, I dropped this thought disorder; gradually, it disappeared from my mind completely.

In my case, colors added a new layer when I was watching television. Television was once just monochrome many years ago. With the invention of color television and Technicolor, television shows became more interesting to watch. Over time, the colors on a television program would become more and more enhanced. With the invention of high-definition TVs and the digital age, I felt like the characters onscreen were trying to hypnotize me and manipulate my thinking. I tried to look away from the person in question, such as an anchor on the nightly news. If I concentrated for a period and looked the anchor straight in the eyes, it would put me in a daze. Could this be linked to the woman with the red eyes?

CHAPTER 7

---•

VACATION AND
REUNION IN 2007

I took my family on a vacation to Atlantis Resorts in Nassau, Bahamas. The resort and island were wonderful. Though I was battling this mental illness, sitting on the sandy beach and watching the waves come in proved comforting to me. We initially had regular rooms but, by luck, got upgraded to a suite with a balcony that overlooked the ocean. However, I would have several incidents during the vacation that did not help my mind.

The first occurred while my family and I were walking down the boardwalk next to the resort. There were many shops and restaurants. At the end of the boardwalk was a calypso drum band playing music. I was with my family when we walked toward the band and looked around at the shops. When I turned back toward the family, they were gone. I quickly got anxious and worried that they had disappeared. I walked into the stores in the area, thinking they might have gone into one the stores. Yet, I could not find them.

After approximately fifteen minutes, I located them in the same area where I had lost them. My anxiety and thought process were elevated and did not go away. As such, the rest of the evening was miserable because of this incident.

The second incident occurred when I was lying by the pool at the resort. My daughter was playing in the water and came across another girl around her age. The girl sounded British, judging from her accent. I had turned away from looking at them for a moment and then turned back to look at my daughter; she was holding a baby doll or a Barbie in her hands, and she and the other girl were playing with it.

I knew that, when I had turned to look away, there had been no dolls in or around the pool. Yet, my daughter suddenly had a doll. My mind started to speed up. Where in the world had this doll come from? When we were leaving, my daughter gave the other girl the doll to keep, which I felt good about, though I had no clue where it had even come from. I thought about this incident with the doll for the rest of the day and vacation.

The last incident I had involved the sea aquarium at the resort. There were plenty of fish, turtles, and large sharks. However, I saw a sharklike creature with a long snout or mouth with many teeth. Of course, this was a type of fish that can be found around the world. But in my mind, I thought it was a prehistoric fish. It looked like something out of the Jurassic period. I even told my wife, "That looks like a prehistoric fish." By now, my mind was already full of delusional thoughts, and this just added to it. It was difficult to stay focused on the vacation and not on the thought disorders and delusions.

In summer 2007, I had my twenty-year high school reunion. There was a tour of the high school and then a get-together at a local bar, which was followed by a formal dinner the next night at the Topeka Country Club. The evening at the bar left me confused. I can picture the classmates I saw that evening, but when they were talking to me, I could not register their names. My wife and I did not stay long at the bar because she was not feeling well. I also did not feel well, and before we left, I was alone and not talking to anyone.

The next morning, I got up early to play a round of golf with some friends. However, I did not enjoy it at all. I believe it was because I had consumed alcohol the night before and had to get up quite early that morning. By the end of the golf round, I just wanted to get back home and take a nap.

The dinner event at the country club was a nice get-together with most of the 1987 class. We sat at a table to eat some of the buffet food and talked a little bit with the people sitting at the same table. After dinner, my mind started to get overwhelmed. My thoughts were racing, and it made me sick to my stomach. I sat in the hallway away from everyone and tried to get it under control, but I couldn't. I left the party shortly thereafter with my wife, and when I got home, I lay on the couch for the rest of the evening.

CHAPTER 8

LEFT SIDE, RIGHT SIDE, AND BACK SIDE

My living room consists of two main chairs facing the television. One of the chairs is on the left side of the television, and the other is on the right. If I sit in the right chair, my head has to turn to the left in order to watch TV. It amazed me and blew my mind that the people on the television screen would look at me in a manner that suggested they were staring straight at me, depending on the seat I was in. So, if I was sitting in the left chair and looking to my right, the person's head on the television would be turned to the right. I did not have any chairs in the middle of the room but would sometimes stand there behind the chairs. Sure enough, the person would be looking straight at me. I took this even further in my delusional state. Could the anchors be reporting the news based on the seat I was sitting in when I was watching television? Were they not only getting these stories from my eyes but also from my ears? I tried to analyze this delusion some more by breaking it down into sides.

I could never understand the reasoning behind this madness in my head. I was constantly trying to read people's facial expressions on the television and trying to find something that would confirm my disorders and delusional thoughts. The same goes for when I would watch the weather forecast; I would be looking for any word or expression, such as smiling or coughing, that would bring my mind to an elevated state.

Could there possibly be three different things happening to me at any given time? Could there be someone on my left side, my right side, and behind me? I thought it impossible.

Over the years, I used to think that people in a restaurant would be looking at me from the left and from the right. I also felt eyes staring at me from behind. This irritated me at times. I would think, *Who are these people?* and *Get out of my head.* In the morning, afternoon, and evening I would think there were different people on my left, right, and behind me. Having this delusional thought was hard for me to handle at times. It was difficult to ignore the feeling that someone was looking at me or at a specific side of me.

There was another game in my head. When I would go out with my wife, I would wonder where she would choose to sit and on which side, especially when it was in an auditorium. Would she sit to my right or would she sit to my left?

I would also have an issue regarding the side of my feet. My left foot would bother me from time to time and felt numb only on the left side. I never experienced any problems with my right foot. This is noteworthy, because, in my mind, I thought this was happening because someone was on my left side.

Working on the computer at home was frustrating at times. We bought a Mac computer several years ago, and I found it a little more difficult to use. On many occasions, something strange would happen when I would be looking at the computer screen. Sometimes the screen would enlarge so I could only see a part of the screen. It was like writing in twelve-point font and then having it jump to thirty-six-point font and seeing only a part of the document. I could not explain why this would happen, but my mind surely came up with something crazy.

I thought maybe part of me, either the left or right side, was some type of robot that could enlarge the information.

Sometimes it would get larger on the left side of the screen, and sometimes on the right side. I also experienced this zoom when I was writing on my PC laptop. It didn't matter if I was on the internet or working with an Excel spreadsheet.

This was one of the top delusional issues I had during these years. My mind would dive into thinking of the Mercedes emblem or the BMW emblem. Both car manufacturers were based in Stuttgart, Germany. The Mercedes emblem had three spokes representing four hours on a clock. One spoke was at twelve and the other two were at four and eight. The BMW emblem, on the other hand, was divided into four portions, with each portion representing three hours. It would represent twelve, three, six, and nine on a clock. My fixation on these symbols would have my mind thinking that there was something behind the numbers and colors. Adding even further to this delusion was the fact there is "Des" in Mercedes, which as I've mentioned previously, related to my grandmother who lived in Des Plaines, Illinois.

It wasn't until late 2016 and into 2017 that I would finally conquer this problem. By that point, it no longer mattered to me if people were still staring at me from any side. I simply kept my mind focused on what I was doing at the time. This had happened to me many times, and sometimes, I would get a quick glimpse of someone staring at me. As I would slowly turn toward whoever was staring, I would catch only about a second of the person turning his or her head away.

On top of this issue, I was also hearing things from both ears. It might be even just a word, but this happened many times. I would hear words such as "no" or "stop" over the years. I would hear things while at the store or at restaurants that I often went to. If someone next to me was having a conversation, I would start hearing words that made no sense and think the people conversing were only there to mess with my mind. This occurred many times in restaurants around Topeka.

I also felt that people did not want me there. This feeling could be triggered by a conversation that I heard or the way one of the waitstaff looked at me when we were waiting to seated. I began to only go through drive-throughs or opt for takeout so I would not experience that feeling.

I would hear animals in the attic—animals large enough to make some noise, like raccoons. I would walk around the house and even on the roof to look for them. But every entry point was closed, so nothing of that size could have ever been in the attic. Upon hearing the noise, I used to think it was a demon or something crawling around the attic.

There was something interesting about the house other than the noises I heard or the animals in the attic. I thought some parts of the house were portals to other areas of the house. In my mind, one could go into the laundry room and end up in the main bedroom.

I could never prove any of these delusions. There was once a mouse in the main bedroom, so I let my cat into the room to try to find it. The mouse ran under the dresser in the corner of the bedroom. I lifted the dresser, tilting it back so the cat could go under it to get the mouse. The cat went behind the dresser. But while I was watching him, he vanished from that spot. Prior to that moment, I had been watching him to be certain that he would be safe when I lowered the dresser back to the ground. However, the next thing I knew, he was walking through the hallway of the main bedroom. In my mind, that corner was some mysterious gateway, like the Bermuda Triangle.

I related this incident in my mind to something that had happened to me while I was in bed. The same incident occurred on two different nights. On the first night, I was on my side of the bed, facing the dresser with my eyes closed. I saw a white light like a ghost coming from the dresser, and it walked up to me. At that moment, I turned to my other side with my back now facing the dresser, and another ghost was walking toward my back. I could not see anything other than the white light, but I sensed that it was behind me and coming from the dresser. On another night, it happened again while I was facing the dresser. This only happened on these two occasions and never again.

It would be a couple of months later that I would have another vision while trying to fall asleep. This vision was of a person standing in a line full of people. To me, it looked like the people standing in line had already passed away and were waiting to enter some place. It was dark, so I assumed this was the line to go to hell. The person I was looking at was brought in closer in my mind's view—so close that I could see his mouth had turn into that of a fanged demon creature.

I also occasionally could smell things that did not make any sense to me at the time. I would walk outside and smell snow in the middle of the summer. I would smell perfume at home, yet I was the only person in the house. I could smell food that seemed to be miles away. I could smell a cigarette in a vehicle that was ahead of me while my own windows were closed. I did not think much about the cigarettes or the other smells, like I did with my other delusions and disorders. I would just think about it for a short time and then start thinking about another delusion or thought disorder.

I cannot talk about the visions, delusions, and thought disorders I had without talking about the main person who I thought was behind my mental illness. For many years, I believed that the mastermind behind my illness and everything associated with it was the devil. I also thought that the delusions and disorders were specifically being generated by him, and he was trying to get me to make a mistake or do something drastic like commit suicide.

There had been several times over the years that I would be watching television and a show would come on that talked about the devil. During one show, it was said that the devil would be chained to the ground by an angel for a thousand years. After the thousand years, he would be released for a season, and then he would be thrown into a lake of fire. On another show, it was mentioned that he would not go into the lake of fire but be thrown in a dark hole forever.

Then I started thinking about the New Testament and the Old Testament. Egyptians and Moses were related to the Ten Commandments. Could the Ten Commandments refer to ten years? Could breaking one of the Ten Commandments result in my staying in this delusional hell forever? My knowledge of the Old and New Testament came primarily from watching television shows on these topics. The Old Testament involved Moses and the Jewish people, and the Ark of the Covenant involved the Ten Commandments tablets.

That got me thinking about the history of civilization and how far back it might go. I thought, *What if the world and civilizations were a lot older than just 5000 BCE?* I began to wonder how old this world could be, and this fired up the thought disorders going on in my head. What if there was an Atlantis or aliens on this earth around the time of the dinosaurs? I did not have a single fact to back up any of the disorders or delusions. My mind just kept focusing on the possibility of aliens or people living during the time of the dinosaurs. To try to back these things up, I would attempt to reference my knowledge of the television shows and movies that I had watched over the years. My mind would not let these delusions go and would continually bring them up, especially if triggered by a word I'd heard someone utter.

At the same time, I would also think about God's master plan, wherein he would finally send the devil to the lake of fire. I would then think the devil was just using me as the scapegoat while he did bad things. It crossed my mind that maybe the mean people I interacted with were mean because of the devil or that they didn't have any choice but to be mean. If it was possible to have my left, right, and back represent different people, then it would certainly be possible for one of these sides, specifically the back, to represent the devil.

I have never discussed these thoughts with anybody, not even my wife. As it has been in many stories, good always triumphs over evil. Maybe the better I feel mentally, the closer I am brought to good and the further I am removed away from evil.

CHAPTER 9

THE START OF THE FINANCIAL CRISIS AND MY INVESTING

The start of the financial crisis in the United States came to a head in fall 2008. The processes of loaning money to people with bad credit or zero down payment caused a major default on mortgage-backed securities for banks. This crisis affected the country's largest banks and largest insurers. Since the insurers were backing a potential default, they were also in a financial crisis. Ultimately, the federal government was required to step in and help the banks and insurers.

During fall 2008, my mind was on other things, as opposed to what was going on with the country's market. At the time, my profit sharing portfolio with the construction company included a high percentage of cash in a money market account. I lost money from my mutual fund and individual stocks just like everyone else in the country. With the market taking a nosedive, nothing was safe except money in money market accounts. The interest rates in money market accounts went down, but the principal was still there. I did not do anything with this account until spring 2009.

In the spring, about a week after the stock market rose again, I invested in five companies. In my mind, the probability of a downturn was possible, but the five companies I invested in were enormous and very profitable. The five companies included Berkshire Hathaway A shares, Microsoft, Google, Wal-Mart, and Exxon Mobil. I purchased 1 share of Berkshire, 300 shares of Microsoft, 15 shares of Google, 50 shares of Walmart, and 75 shares of Exxon. To be more specific, I tried to buy 15.151515 shares of Google, and 75.757575 shares of Exxon Mobil. I later found out that shares aren't dealt in fractions. It had to be 15 shares and 75 shares. I calculated the market capitalization of the five companies before investing in them. At the time, their market capitalization was over $900 billion. When I made my investments, the stock market was on the rise. I believed they were solid investments, and they would keep rising.

After a couple of weeks, my mind developed a delusion, making my investing something much greater. Was my investing in these five companies causing the stock market to rise? I started to think about the billions of dollars in each company's market capitalization and the impact they would have on the overall market. The five companies I invested in were not all in one sector, but rather were oil and gas and retail conglomerates and computer-related companies. I started to monitor the Dow Jones 30 index. There I would find three of the five companies I'd invested in. The Standard & Poor's and Nasdaq were rising, but I did not look at them as closely as I did the Dow Jones.

I would listen to CNBC during the evening and would try to pick up any information related to my delusional thinking. I would pay attention to any report related to the five companies. My hypomania would increase with any misplaced word. I even watched television shows to find information.

In February 2012, I sold 25 shares of Exxon Mobil and bought 25 shares of AT&T. At the time, I was right in believing AT&T had a better dividend. Somehow, my mind took off in another direction, and I started looking at my transactions on a much larger scale—instead of 25 shares I started to think it was 25 percent of Exxon Mobil with a market cap of well over $400 billion. With this 25 percent, or $100 billion, I believed I had invested $30 billion in AT&T and bought stock in Goldman Sachs at around $25 billion. I also believed I'd purchased roughly $4 billion of Facebook stock, $9 billion in Barrick Gold, and 8 billion in URS Corporation—an engineering and construction company based in San Francisco. I named these companies "the 200 share companies" because I had 200 shares in them. The total I believed I had was $75 billion. Since the $100 billion would be taxed at 15 percent, there would be $15 billion in taxes. That left about $10 billion in cash and not stock. Of that amount, $5 billion went to the state, which would have taken the cash down to around $5 billion.

AT&T was up several dollars from when I'd bought the shares but was still paying over 5 percent in dividends. Goldman Sachs' stock price has risen over the years, and Barrick Gold went down because the price of gold dropped. URS was bought by AECOM, so I have shares in AECOM now. Finally, Facebook has shot off like a rocket. Shares are around $175 per share, and I purchased them for a little over $19 per share.

I even had a solution for gold dropping in price. I started to think I could create a mountain of gold. I ran some numbers on the total value and it came to about $2 trillion. I even set up the Barrick Gold company in a way that would have it mining around $40 billion of gold per year and making a profit after purchasing equipment, with labor costs of around $20 billion. I tied equipment costs to mining equipment companies such as Caterpillar. A few billion dollars would go to other companies, but the bulk of the $5 billion to $10 billion would be through Caterpillar, specifically its mining division. In my mind, this constituted yearly equipment allocation. Equipment that was not needed for gold would go to mining other materials. In addition, in my mind, an allocation of a minimum of $5 billion was made for purchasing other mines that produce other ores along with gold. Labor costs were around $5 billion a year for the people in the offices and at the mines.

This is just one example of the way my mind was working. My mind could set up a multibillion-dollar company in a matter of one hour or less. Of course, there was no way a company could make those kinds of profits, and there was no mountain of gold to mine. But at that time, I believed there was a company.

Also, in my delusions, I could not look at the name Standard & Poor's without making a connection to Standard—the name of the Rockefeller company.

It wasn't until spring 2014 and my resignation from the company that these thoughts would completely disappear, as I had to sell some shares and remove some money from my IRA. I sold the one share in Berkshire A and others from the five companies.

Nowadays, I pay very little attention to the five companies. I still sometimes watch CNBC during the day, but I don't have the delusion that I am the smartest person on the planet. In fact, watching these shows and listening to people talk about charts and options goes in one ear and out the other. So much technology has gone into investing. I am sure all the new gadgets do a good job, but it ultimately comes down to the investor. Nowadays, I just look to see if the market is up or down. There was nothing like having to sell shares in one of the five companies to put everything into perspective and break free from that continual delusion.

CHAPTER 10

RECOGNIZING A VISION

In 2009, I continued to battle my illness. I kept myself busy at work and with helping around the house and with the kids. I went to a 3-D movie at the movie theater with my daughter in February. At the beginning of the movie, I had a thought disorder, along with a delusional experience. I believed the movie could help children with autism. At the very beginning, when words on the screen came up, I thought my eyes were pulling them closer, triggering my delusion. While the movie was playing, I could not let go of the thought that it could help children with autism. This thought disorder stuck around in my mind for months.

Later, when we would go see a newly released 3-D movie, I would try to put myself inside the movie. Virtual reality has been gaining more popularity over the past several years. With virtual reality, you are in the middle of something happening, whether you are walking down a street in some city or country or fighting alien robots. I was experiencing this in the movie theater at that time.

In March, I went to an Eagles concert in Kansas City with my wife. At the Eagles concert, I had a new delusion—this time involving the sound from the concert and how it would bounce off the inside of the Sprint Center and amplify the effect I was experiencing. To believe I had something to do with the sound was ridiculous. But at that time, I believed I controlled the sound.

In May, our construction company was working with a local client. One day, I was driving around the back of the plant and felt a little more tired than usual. I pulled over to the back of the plant, and with the engine running, I closed my eyes for a brief period and had another vision. This vision was not like the others, and I haven't seen it since. I saw a group of ghosts flying around in different directions, and one of them flew close to my face and faced me straight on, like looking in a mirror. Its face was a pale, its eyes were black, and its mouth was closed shut like someone had sewn it. I saw the ghost for a few seconds and then opened my eyes. I did not understand the meaning of this vision. Who were these ghosts, and what did they have to do with me?

I closed my eyes once more and saw another vision, this one of a woman in a witch's hat, which quickly disappeared from my view as I opened my eyes again. Over the years, these kinds of visions would randomly enter my mind and give me a fright. There was nothing like trying to go to sleep and having a vision of a demon for a second or two. This happened on more than one occasion, and it would startle me.

During this time, I would wonder when the visions would stop. Surely they had to stop someday, but this thought only made things worse. I would think that this day would be the day or this night would be the night. And every morning I would wake up to another day, and nothing had changed. I was not alone in thinking this. I believe others with mental illnesses think the same thing. Even people without a mental illness have these thoughts after a bad day. It just boils down to a sense of feeling powerless and not in control of anything.

In the summer, the family took a trip to Branson, Missouri, to see the sights and attend a show. The five-hour drive to Branson was miserable because of the problems in my head, so I ended up speeding to try to get there sooner.

I did not know what to expect at Branson and was surprised at how many people lived in the city, especially along the main road where the traffic was backed up for miles. Fortunately, the hotel was close to the exit, so we did not hit any traffic after arriving. We stayed in an older hotel, and I spent a lot of time trying to stop myself from thinking that if there was an earthquake, we would probably not survive.

We visited the *Titanic* museum and the butterfly sanctuary, but the journey took about an hour because of the traffic. During the trip, I had many thought disorders going on in my mind. I toured the *Titanic* museum thinking other people could hear my thoughts. At the butterfly sanctuary, I was paranoid that I was going to step on a butterfly.

One afternoon, I was feeling terrible. The feeling I had was like what I'd experienced during my high school reunion. My head felt overwhelmed, and I had to lie in bed for the entire afternoon. My wife and kids went to a rock climbing wall while I rested.

I felt better in the evening, so we went to see a magic show in Branson that was just as good as the ones in Las Vegas. I took my medication while watching the show, and afterward, we stood in line to meet the magicians and get a picture with them. It took a while to make our way to them, but it was extremely uncomfortable for me because we were in a group of people standing in line. I had no control over my thoughts, and they certainly worked me over that night. I was relieved on the trip back to the hotel.

The drive back home to Topeka was a little easier than the drive to Branson had been. I did not speed on the way back. The point during the trip back at which I knew we were getting closer to home was when we drove through Truman Lake. I experienced fewer thought disorders, primarily because we were heading to our home. I slept well the first night back because I was in my bed.

The afternoon of August 11, 2009, I was watching my son play football. He was new to playing football, and for some reason, I heard the coach say, "Nice stop." I looked at him and the team and developed yet another disorder in my head. I started to believe my son was a lot better at playing football than what I was seeing. I always felt I was somehow missing something, whether it was a football play or something on television. I thought about this for the rest of the day, and then it disappeared with the vision in the evening.

That evening, I had a vision when I was trying to sleep. The vision was of Adolf Hitler sitting in a chair with his uniform on and his legs crossed. The vision first started from a distance of more than ten feet. He was then magnified to the point where he disappeared after the magnification reached his right eye. It was like using a movie camera to show a wider view and a close-up aimed at his right eye. This vision was several seconds long, and I immediately opened my eyes after seeing it. Up until this point, I had never recognized anyone from my visions. I eventually fell asleep after having the vision, but it felt like several hours had passed before I slept.

The next morning, and for many years to come, my mind would play that vision over and over. I would later associate this vision with the things l have written about in this book, such as the Olympics and television. This vision put plenty of delusional thoughts into my head.

Early in September, around Labor Day, I took the first of several trips up to

North Platte, Nebraska, to spend time with a couple of friends from high school. We traveled north from North Platte to a place not far from South Dakota near the town of Valentine. We were headed on a tanking trip down the creek. Aside from my delusions and thought disorders, the trip was fun. On the ride, we stopped several times along the creek to explore the banks and swim in the water. At the end of the trip, we camped by the water, drank, and smoked cigars. My friends would reminisce about high school, and I recall having a very hard time remembering what they were talking about. It was practically impossible for me to try to remember something that far back. Talking about the old times made me feel left out of the conversation.

During the night, we cooked dinner and sat around the camp area talking. I was not as overweight on this trip as I would later become, so physically, I did not feel too bad; mentally, though, I was a wreck. The thought disorders racing through my mind—specifically the thought that my friends knew what I was thinking—led me to keep quiet and not participate in the conversation. At home I used a CPAP (continuous positive airway pressure) machine to help me sleep, and camping without it left me restless. I did not have any visions on this trip, but I did have visions of two heads floating around on a later trip.

Future tanking trips included the kids, and by the time the last tanking trip came around, I felt mentally and physically miserable; my weight had ballooned to over 360 pounds. I would occasionally smile during these trips, but I was never genuinely having a good time.

In October 2009, my wife and I took a trip to New York City. I had never been to New York before, so I was excited to see the city. When we arrived, we took a taxi to the hotel, which happened to be located next to the World Trade Center, so we could see the Freedom Tower from our window. Several events triggered delusions and thought disorders during this trip.

The first thought disorder took place as I was walking from the hotel toward a local sandwich shop. Not only was the hotel located next to the World Trade Center, it was also right next to one of the oldest churches in the city. While we were walking to the sandwich shop, a man walked by and held up a picture of the World Trade Center on fire. My initial reaction was shock. Then I started to think, and I began to associate the vision of Hitler I'd had on August 11, 2009, with the event in 2001, which made me sick to my stomach. I prayed to God the thought would leave my mind. We went to the sandwich shop—which was filled with pictures of people during that terrible day—and then walked to the church next door and looked at the 9/11 memorabilia.

We took the subway to get to places like Rockefeller Center and Times Square; we ate at the Olive Garden in Times Square and toured Rockefeller Center. The Christmas tree was up but wasn't fully decorated yet. We also saw a Broadway show that created another delusion.

We sat in the middle row during the show, and at one point, one of the performers on stage looked right at me. I thought she was looking at me and no one else. This thought raced through my mind the rest of the night but, fortunately, did not gain any traction.

On one of our subway trips, we ended up at the Bloomingdale's entrance. I looked at my wife, and she seemed confused as to where we were and wondered whether this the way to Bloomingdale's. For some reason, I started to believe it was the entrance from the subway. We entered Bloomingdale's at the basement level, and music was playing. At that point, I started to believe that the subway had somehow been changed to add an entrance to the department store.

When we took the subway again back to the hotel, my left ear was ringing. When we were ready to board the subway, it was packed with people, so we caught a cab back to the hotel instead. Because of the noise in my left ear, I started to wonder whether the subway had been completely changed, along with the entrances. In addition, two things happened that reinforced my delusions: The subway we rode later looked as though it was on a new line or route. And when we were back at the hotel and had a drink at the bar, the bartender asked my wife if anything had changed during our time in the city.

One evening in New York City, my wife and I went to eat at a restaurant. During the meal, a couple walked by us, and I could have sworn the man said my name to the woman. Believing I had heard my name set me off; I was thinking all sorts of things. How would he know my name? This was New York, not Topeka. If he knew my name, then some of the previous thought disorders and delusions would be proven correct. Luckily, it did not set me off into a manic state, as that would have ruined the rest of our trip.

The last delusional thought I had during this trip happened when we were driving to the airport on our way home to Kansas. I noticed a large power plant located near a river and thought it was odd that no smoke was coming from the stacks. It was October, and the temperatures were mild, but usually one can see smoke if the plant is in operation. I started to believe the power plant was not running, and all the power in the entire city was being generated through my mind.

CHAPTER 11

THIS SOUNDS LIKE ENERGY

Early in 2009, I started hearing things. I started to hear a humming sound like that of an electrical generator. It was difficult to determine whether it was coming from one side of my head or the other, or whether it was coming from behind me. In the beginning, the sound was loud, but over the years, it became less loud. I started to believe that I was moving in waves so rapidly that I was generating electricity. My delusions made me believe I was a power plant.

A delusion that was developed because of the previous one involved the size of everything. I started to believe that everything was so small it would not take a lot of electricity to generate the power needed. As I had with all the other thought disorders and delusions, I would search for things on the television or in the newspaper that would confirm my thoughts. The construction company I worked for upgraded old substations; could this have anything to do with what I was thinking?

I also started to see an electrical power volt moving around in circles like electrons and protons. The humming sound never caused any harm though. I could only hear it when I was in a quiet area and could concentrate on it.

Later, the delusions caused by the humming sound would take on a new level. When I would look out over the city of Topeka and concentrate on something that had lights, such as the Frito-Lay plant, the lights began to look brighter. When this was happening, some of the lights from the cars driving down the road would flicker on and off. This would occur many times over the years, mostly when I drank. I believed the humming sound in my head was causing this to happen.

One night when it was raining, I was looking at the local substation wires from my bedroom window. To me, the rain on the door looked like it was running off the overhead power wires, and it looked like the high voltage lines were sparking. After I saw this, I tried to fall asleep but saw what seemed like people riding an escalator up to somewhere. I thought maybe they were going up to heaven.

The delusions related to power increased over time. At some point, I believed I could pull the moon closer to the earth because I felt like I could do anything. I would then look at the stars and try to pull them closer as well.

January 4, 2010, is one of several dates I remember vividly. That night I had a vision of two witches surrounded by symbols. It only took a few seconds to see this, but what I saw after was strange. A vortex started to suck the symbols and witches in, resulting in a black space. I could not explain this vision. Were the witches trying to put a spell together to bring someone back? What stood out about this vision was that it was animated. It was in color and made me feel like I was watching a television show. This type of vortex vision occurred one other time on January 11, 2012.

On January 11, 2010, when I tried to fall asleep, I saw a person looking downward. I can only describe it as someone coming up from a place below. He had a smile on his face and had long brown hair. I did not recognize him but thought maybe he was a saint. Additionally, a pattern started to develop related to certain dates, in which I was almost certain something would happen on specific dates. As it turned out, this was not the case.

In the summer 2010, the family took a trip to Washington, DC. My son was taking part in a leadership conference for about a week, so we dropped him off at the conference and then spent the week looking at monuments and attractions. During our stay in Washington, DC, we stayed at the L'Enfant Hotel close to some of the main monuments. Such as the Lincoln, Jefferson, and Washington monuments and a couple of museums. My mental state remained the same, with delusions and thought disorders.

The subway system located below the hotel in Washington got me thinking about the New York subway system. The subway in Washington was new and looked like it was built recently. I started thinking that maybe this station had not been built by construction workers but with my mind. My paranoia about others hearing what I was thinking added to this delusion.

During the trip, we drove out to the Udvar-Hazy airplane museum to look at the airplanes. In addition, we went to Arlington Cemetery to look at the Tomb of the Unknown Soldier, along with the grave of John Kennedy and other former presidents. The air museum was interesting because there was an SR-71 spy plane on display. This would be significant in my delusions; twisting the display into another delusional, my thoughts had me believing I was somehow involved with Lockheed Martin, the company that built the plane. There wasn't a major company in the country I didn't think my grandparents were associated with. I remember thinking some of these thoughts when we toured the museum, but I tried my best to control my thoughts.

There was a large group of people at the Tomb of the Unknown Soldier, so I spent most the time making sure I did not think any crazy thought that they could possibly hear.

I would also always try to connect banks to my grandparents. For example, located next door to the White House was a Bank of America building. Bank of America was, of course, from Charlotte, North Carolina, and had branches in Topeka. In my mind, I would attempt to put this information together and to tie it to my grandparents.

The family took another trip, this one to Albuquerque, New Mexico. On this trip, we met up with my wife's brother and his wife. We went on this trip to visit my wife's uncle, who had lived in Albuquerque for many years. During this trip, several delusional thoughts entered my mind.

On a visit to Applebee's, there was a lot of commotion as to where my son was going to sit. As this was happening, I had a quick vision of a demon woman. I shook it off, but it had affected me enough that I had to wait in the car for my family to finish saying their goodbyes inside the restaurant. An interesting part about that dinner was the introduction to the word "steal"—the waiter had said, "Let me steal that from you," in reference to taking something from me. I heard that word many times over the years and would relate it to somebody stealing something or to Andrew Carnegie, the founder of US Steel.

Along with the Rockefellers and Vanderbilts, I thought of Andrew Carnegie every time that word was used. In 2016 and 2017, the word would no longer trigger this in me, but it would make me smile at the torment it had caused me.

By the end of the trip, I'd had my fill of the city. We met over at my wife's uncle's house for dinner, and I felt isolated the whole night because of the ongoing delusional thoughts in my mind.

On the trip back to Topeka, I had no relief in my mind. I told myself I would never visit Albuquerque again. Albuquerque was a nice city, but my memories lay in the mental experiences I had while there.

At times, I would almost feel there was an invisible barrier around Topeka as I entered the city. When I would be on the outskirts of Topeka, my ears would ring. This happened more than once. When traveling to another place and returning to Topeka, I would wonder whether I was entering Topeka or a completely different place. I believed I was in some type of machine that was able to manipulate and change the sights faster than the blink of an eye.

CHAPTER 12

VACATIONS IN 2011

The beginning of 2011 was rough because my mother passed away on February 21, and I took the news hard. She had been in an assisted facility for several years leading up to her passing. I would try to see her once a week during those years, usually on a Sunday, to bring her food or coffee. She liked McDonald's coffee, so I would order it from the drive-through, making sure there were three creams and three sugars in it. She did not get out of bed much while she stayed at the facility. I assume she didn't have the drive needed to get out of bed and be more mobile.

The days leading up to her passing were extremely sad for me. Not only was I struggling with my mental illness, I was also sad and depressed, given her condition. I cried several times while I sat by her bed while she was in a bad state, and I held her hand and kissed her forehead the day before she passed away. She was a good mother over the years and always tried to be involved in my life.

There was a small funeral service, with only family members in attendance. I make sure there are flowers on her grave at least twice a year because she loved flowers.

During this time, my mental illness continued.

In July, I had another vision of a person traveling down an escalator, but this was not an escalator at a department store. The vision appeared to be very close and would later recede into the distance. The person on the escalator had a glow around his head, as though he was wearing a hat made from light bulbs. The second view of the vision seemed to have me looking at the escalator from above some buildings and watching the same person descend toward the buildings below. I believed this person was traveling from heaven to hell and wondered whether he could be St. John the Baptist or even Jesus. To this day, I can recall this vision.

The family took a vacation to Las Vegas, and we stayed at the New York-New York Hotel & Casino and went to see Hoover Dam. Two delusions occurred on this trip as well.

The first delusion occurred when we were walking through the MGM Grand Hotel & Casino. We were walking through a hallway, and when I looked to my left, I thought I saw some kind of dog creature. The creature looked me right in the eyes, but when I turned back to look at it, all I saw was a statue inside the casino.

The second delusion came when we crossed the bridge between New York-New York and the MGM casino. My daughter picked up a nickel off the ground and gave it to a homeless man. Later, as we were eating at the Circus Circus casino buffet, I saw someone who looked homeless taking food from the buffet. I started to believe homeless people in Las Vegas were treated to a meal.

I didn't gamble in Las Vegas because I didn't find it interesting. Nor did I think I'd win—and there was no fun for me in losing.

A shuttle was supposed to take us to the airport, but something went wrong, and we ended up having to pay for a taxi instead. When things like that happen on vacation, it ruins the experience, but my vacations were always ruined because of my delusions.

On August 21, I had another vision of a person's face with a bloody mouth. It looked like he had gotten into a fight with someone and had been hit in the mouth. It only entered my mind for a few seconds, but it was just long enough to get a good look at him. What appeared next was strange; a pair of wolf eyes emerged from the middle of my line of vision and moved up and away. I instantly opened my eyes and wondered if it was someone I knew.

On September 13, I saw the first of a series of visions that would occur on the same date each year. Certain dates during my twelve years had a higher probability of something happening, whether it was hearing something or seeing something in a vision. This vision was of a child—a child who looked like a criminal. It floated into the background and then floated to the left and behind a wall. I instantly wondered if I had just seen a rue. I don't even know what a rue was, aside from hearing the word. There are several streets in New Orleans that have that name.

We took a trip with the family to Chicago in fall 2011. I'd been to Chicago several times over the years, and I always liked the city. The people were friendly, and there were plenty of museums and sights to see. On this trip, we walked the Miracle Mile with all the shops and businesses. We stopped at the multilevel flagship American Girl store, where my wife and daughter stayed while my son and I went to the Apple Store. This was my first time in an Apple Store.

We spent time in the store playing around with the computers. I always believed I knew more about computers than I actually did, and while at the Apple Store, I opened the calculator application and starting punching in random numbers for the calculator to compute. In my mind, I was programming the computer.

We then met up with the girls again and stopped inside one of the oldest pump stations in the city. The woman who worked there told us the place was haunted, and all I could think about the rest of the trip was whether I would see the ghost. We left the pump station and entered the Hershey store to look around and then decided to eat something at the Ghirardelli's, which was across the street.

We spent a majority of our time at the main museums in Chicago. The T. rex skeleton at the Field Museum was interesting to see, and its McDonald's sponsorship made it even more interesting. I wondered whether there was some significance to the sponsorship. I tried to piece something together, but nothing came out of it other than the thought of my grandparents' involvement. Museums would trigger many thoughts, just because of all the people. We ended up eating at the McDonald's in the museum and traveled to the Museum of Science and Industry.

There is one more site on our Chicago trip I want to mention because of what my mind would try to connect. We took a tour of the Sears Tower. From the observation deck, you could see the city. I looked through one of the binoculars and noticed a McDonald's sign close to a power plant. Seeing these two things together was enough for me to make a connection between power and McDonald's. It didn't look like the power plant was in service anymore, but that only added to my delusions. If it was not running, then maybe Chicago was running on another power source?

On the flight back to Topeka, something strange happened. It was dark outside, and in the distance, you could see a large compound of buildings lit up. All the lights on the buildings were flickering, making me believe I had something to do with this just by simply looking at them. This set my mind off again on the delusions related to power.

CHAPTER 13

THE STREET-AND-LETTERS NAME GAME

I titled this chapter "The Street-and-Letters Name Game" because it has everything to do with the streets in Topeka, Kansas, and their relation to the letters of the alphabet. I started associating letters with numbers in late 2011. The alphabet had 26 letters, *A–Z*, with each letter corresponding to a number. For example, the number 17 would be the letter *Q* and so on. I tried to associate these letters with specific thought disorders and delusions.

The visions I saw on September 13 were associated with the letter M. Every month of the year had specific words associated with them. Take June or July, for example. Both these months started with *J* (or 10). Then, I would add the numbers associated with the rest of the letters together. For example, the number for the month of June would be 50—*J* (10) plus *U* (21) plus *N* (14) plus *E* (5), which totals 50. I would work on these numbers and letters numerous times throughout the years. Whenever something came up that involved a word of interest, I would calculate the numbers and the amount.

The same was done with the zip code of Topeka, which started with 666. I lived in the zip code 66610, which added up to 28.

I also associated the letters with numbers to represent time. If there was a *C*, for example, the time was very long ago, while *Z* was not as long. I associated the number 3 with *C*, so I would add 10 to that to get 13 and then 23 by adding another ten. I could manipulate numbers in my head and turn the numbers into many different things.

For example, starting with the last letter in the alphabet, which is *Z* (or 26), the word "Oz" would represent 27 because the *Z* was in the second position. In the word "Nazi," the *Z* is in the third position, so that would make 28. The word "plaza" was 29, with its *Z* in the fourth position, and "Switzerland" was 30, with *Z* occupying the fifth position. I could locate *Z* words all the way up to the number 33.

I tried hard to put letters and words together. I focused a lot of my attention on the *Z* words. I was born on November 27, so did that mean I was the second *Z*? Since Nazi was associated with *Z* and I had a vision of Hitler, was there a connection to all of this somehow? Was I going through all of this because of my place in the alphabet? My mind just knew that this area was a great form of torture, with so many different scenarios that could go on inside my mind.

Furthermore, I started to dissect the street names and numbers in Topeka. Going from north to south, the names of the roads began to have significance, starting with the road named Burlingame. I got married in the church located on this road, and my grandparents lived in an apartment complex on this road in the '80s. Take the *u* out of Burlingame and insert the letter *e*, and you have the capital city of Germany or Berlin.

I would think about Hitler and the important people from that time, including Himmler and Hermann and try to tie their names to the number 8 because their names had an *H* in it. I had lived on 3041 Arnold Street just south of Twenty-Ninth Street in the past. I couldn't leave the numbers 30 and 41 alone and would try to put 30 into years and 41 into years. I didn't have a clue what those numbers represented.

I would also try to put the three main interstate highways—I-70, I-80, and I-90—in this delusion and thought disorder. Those highways were built when Eisenhower was president, and he modeled them off the German Autobahn. I wondered if there could be a connection with these highways. Could the numbers also represent decades in the twentieth century? The name "Caesar" can be manipulated into the word "Sears." I would also wonder why the *a* was ahead of the *e*. While I was working the numbers in my head and trying to find a solution, I would also start to look at the businesses that were located on the roads around Topeka.

I thought there was something hidden in the location of the businesses, especially at major intersections. If you were facing north at the intersection of Twenty-Ninth Street and Wanamaker, there was a strip mall with a British Petroleum station to the right of you and a McDonald's, a bank, and Hy-Vee grocery store to the left. Across the intersection and to the right was a liquor store and, originally, a hardware store. Across the intersection to the left was another bank and a strip mall with a CVS located there. I wondered, If I crossed them in an *X* pattern, did British Petroleum and the CVS have something in common? Did the Hy-Vee and the liquor store have something in common? I would do the same thing at different intersections. These delusions were only giving me more thought disorders. My mind fed off that information and continued to push to new levels of thought disorders. Thinking about numbers was one area that was tough to get under control. Not only did I associate the numbers of streets and businesses in Topeka, but I would also have thought disorders about other states and countries.

Another state that my mind was fixated on was Arkansas, specifically with the first three letters of the name. I wondered whether they named that state after the Ark of the Covenant. Was the city St. Petersburg, Florida, named after St. Petersburg, Russia? I believed it was named after the city in Russia and wondered why it had been so named. The same could be said about Pittsburgh and Manhattan, Kansas. The cities, respectively, were most certainly named after Pittsburgh, Pennsylvania, and Manhattan in New York City.

I tried to dissect the city of Paris with letters and numbers. I looked at this city more than any other city because of a picture of my dad with my grandmother. The picture was taken in Paris, and it was an illustration of the two of them, not a photograph. The picture emphasized their blue eyes and it was created around World War II. Thinking about Paris brought me to think about Napoleon and what he had done during his reign as emperor of France. Dissecting his name, you get "Na," which could be the beginning of Nazi, and in the middle of his name is "Pole." Could this be the North Pole, the South Pole, or Poland? Like Hitler, Napoleon had tried to conquer most of Europe and Russia. In both cases, Adolf Hitler and Napoleon had been defeated when they'd tried to conquer Russia.

I would also start to look at names of businesses that had an apostrophe and the letter *s* attached to them, such as McDonald's or Kohl's. In French, there is a word, "S'." And in the United States, "St." is short for the word "saint." Did the *S'* mean they were dead when they became saints? And did the *'s* mean there was a long period between letters? My mind developed all sorts of thought disorders.

I would take a map and draw a straight edge and line up to the two cities to see if anything could be determined. The only thing I discovered was that Russia to Florida and New York to Kansas went in a southwest direction. I would look at the longitude and latitude of the cities and try to piece something together that would make some sense to me. I would even try to put something together related to the Nazi swastika and the way the black lines ran in a northeast to southwest and northwest to southeast direction, thinking there was more to the swastika than met the eye. It took several years to finally stop having these thought disorders.

CHAPTER 14

FOREVER FALLING DOWN A HOLE

On January 11, 2012, I started off the year with a new vision. I envisioned a person with a growth on the side of his head that resembled a horn. Like in all the other visions, except for that of Adolf Hitler, I had no idea who this person was. And he looked completely different from the man with the long brown hair I had seen in 2010. After I had seen this person, the vision disappeared and was replaced by a cat. The cat was an ordinary house cat, and there was nothing unusual about its appearance. The cat was then sucked into a vortex, and the vision disappeared. I did not understand the cat's significance, unless it was somehow tied to the person.

Later in the summer, the family took a trip to Orlando, Florida, to Disney World and Universal Studios. We stayed at the Hard Rock Hotel, which was within walking distance of the Universal theme park. As we walked through the area filled with restaurants and shops, we stopped in Margaritaville.

While we ate, I began to think the radio station was broadcasting live at this restaurant. Could people listening hear my thoughts over the radio? This threw my mind into another thought disorder. I was not having a good time at the restaurant because my mind did not allow me to.

When we toured the theme park and rode on some of the rides, I was still not having a good time. When I think back on these twelve years, it makes me sad to think just how incapacitated I was by my thoughts and delusions and how I never had any fun with my family on our vacations.

The one ride at Universal Studios that I did enjoy was the Simpsons ride because it made you feel like you were on a roller coaster. I would later start to believe I had something to do with the ride, controlling it using my mind and eyes.

We spent a day at Disney World walking around and going on rides. A shop in Epcot Center had small trees from Japan. For a split second, I thought I had bowed toward one of the miniature trees as though I was someone from Japan. After finishing the day at Disney World, we took a ride back to our rental car.

We shared a tramcar with a couple and their daughter from Germany. My daughter told them that her Opa (grandfather in German) lived in Gutersloh. They were nice and acknowledged that they knew the city. When we arrived at our destination and got off the car, the German man said, "Look, it's the Rhineland." I tried to associate what he said to something related to World War II, but it only made my mind race.

Later in the evening, we ate dinner at a Planet Hollywood restaurant. While waiting for our table, we stood at the bar area, and I saw both bartenders walk out from behind the bar. Within a second, they were back behind the bar, and I saw one of the bartenders take a shot of Jägermeister. One second they were gone, and the next they were back behind the bar. I started to believe I had teleported them from one place to the other.

The maître d' sat us at a booth in the middle of the restaurant. As we ate, the restaurant played music. My mind was already elevated from the bar episode, so I just kept going through the delusion throughout dinner. It got to the point where I thought I was somehow elevating the sound of the music, adding energy to the songs. By the time we left the restaurant, the music was loud, but I overheard a woman say, "Wow." She was just impressed with the restaurant, but in my mind, her exclamation just added to my delusion of believing I had something to do with the music and videos.

We took a trip to see the Kennedy Space Center. While on our way there, we passed a power plant in the distance. I thought that it looked relatively new and started to believe I had somehow just built it. We toured the different launch sites at the space center and ended up at the main building where the space shuttle is retrofitted prior to being driven to the launch pad.

I developed an interest in Wernher von Braun, the German scientist who came to work at NASA after being one of the scientists who developed the jet engines for the Third Reich during World War II. I don't know exactly why I suddenly developed an interest in this man; perhaps it was because of his involvement in World War II, or maybe I was impressed with the fact that he designed rockets for the United States.

I had only one vision on this trip. I envisioned a man with a 1980's haircut wearing a rock concert T-shirt, but I did not recognize his face. Nor did I recognize the band on his T-shirt. I tried to fall asleep after the vision but couldn't. The next day, I thought about the vision, but it only lasted that day.

Several weeks later, after we had returned from Florida, another vision occurred. I was sitting in the recliner chair in the basement on the morning of September 13. I had a vision of myself reflected in a mirror. The face and hair were identical, but the person in front of me did not have a goatee like I had at the time. The man facing me started to disconnect. His entire face and head started to float away in slow motion. It felt like this person was stuck to my left eye, and he had just gotten unstuck. When I saw the man float away, I saw an image of a room with people's heads floating around. I believe this was tied to my visions that contained only people's heads.

One of the floating heads was that of a man with a long mustache, reminiscent of a French man. I thought about the way people were executed years ago in France with guillotines. Could some of these people have been involved in the beheadings that occurred in France? Or was a king trying to get rid of certain people, so he would be safe and remain king for a long time? Could these people be the Des people I talked about earlier? Could I be related to these things somehow?

On October 19, 2012, my wife, some friends, and I attended my twenty-five-year class reunion. It was not a large get-together like the twenty-year reunion, where more than a hundred classmates had been in attendance. At this one, fewer than thirty classmates were there.

As I sat at the table with friends, a strange thing occurred. I glanced to my right side, and my girlfriend from high school handed me a picture. The picture was from high school of me and a friend I played football with in 1985. After handing it to me, she said to give it back to her when we were getting ready to leave. I looked back to the right again, and there was another classmate staring at me. She looked upset. She looked like a photograph. Seconds later, she disappeared.

For the next hour, I sat at the table and talked with the people there. When we were leaving, the picture was returned to my girlfriend from high school. In my mental state, I believed she had appeared out of thin air. I thought about that night for several weeks, but nothing came out of thin air, and the torture my mind experienced was more than enough.

A month later, I had another vision at nighttime. I saw an angel that resembled an animation. There was a black backdrop, and the angel stood there with his wings moving. Then he looked up and flew away. With all my prior visions being of demons and terrible things, I didn't know what to think of this one. It was the first time I had seen something from heaven. I started to think that God was looking down on what was going on with me. I would spend several Tuesdays in the future hoping to see something similar, but nothing good ever materialized.

The final vision of the year involved a man and two entities—I say two entities because they had no form and looked like ghosts. The man looked as though he'd been pushed through a door and was falling down a dark hole with his legs and arms stretched out. The dark hole around him moved with static, so it looked like he was stationary when falling. I did not recognize the man, but I believed he would be falling forever. Was this some type of punishment for the man? Or was something else going on, like he was being kept from aging, the fall stopping time for him? There were always plenty of scenarios I could come up with in my mind.

CHAPTER 15

THE ALIEN VISIONS AND TATTOO PEOPLE

Not all my visions were of people or things that looked like they came from hell. Several visions were of aliens, which made me think I was losing my mind. The visions I had of different aliens are beyond words. While I was trying to fall asleep one night, two visions appeared one after the other. The first vision included people dancing, with cliffs in the background. The people had the same facial features as humans, but their heads were elongated. The color of the background color was a warm yellow with some red. The vision only lasted a couple of seconds.

Another vision consisted of miniature people dressed in winter clothes. It seemed as though the power was turned on when I had this vision. There was snow on the ground, and one of the people had his butt shaking back and forth. This vision also only lasted a couple of seconds.

I had another vision involving an alien who I only saw from the belly up. The alien's eyes were much larger than human eyes, and the top of his head was round and hairless. The alien resembled the "typical" aliens we see in movies. In addition, a man with long brown wavy hair emerged and sat behind an old-fashioned wooden desk stacked with paper and pens. As I stared at the man, he began to shake his head to signal no. I quickly opened my eyes and wondered why he was shaking his head at me. Was the vision of the alien off limits and never meant to happen? I then started to believe I was an alien visiting earth and living in Topeka. I didn't understand who the man behind the desk was and wondered if he was the devil or God.

Another alien vision I experienced included the coolest looking alien by far. The alien had a flat head and his entire head was red. The alien looked rather large, and I assumed he was a soldier because he was wearing armor and was holding a laser gun. The armor was made up of rectangular metal bands that were much longer than they were wide. The armor looked as though it could deflect a round of bullets. I started to wonder why he was dressed in a battle suit and carrying a weapon. Was he getting ready to fight someone?

The vision I had included one image after the other. The first thing I saw was a fight scene that resembled jet fighters attacking the spaceship along with the alien spacecraft. In the next vision, I was standing on the deck of a large submarine. A couple of soldiers dropped down on the top of the deck and were wearing sophisticated uniforms. Their helmets covered most of their faces, along with their heads. I opened the hatch, and a person with long hair was on the ladder. I reached out my hand to help him out of the submarine. After I helped him out of the submarine, the vision disappeared, and I saw an alien that resembled a fish with whiskers. It was hard to see all the features of the alien because the picture in my mind was upside down. All these visions took less than five seconds to see, but they felt much longer. I thought maybe there was a war somewhere, and I was only seeing a part of the war. With no reference to time, it could have happened way in the future or in the past. I couldn't stop wondering who these aliens were.

The last alien vision came in the form of a robot alien with a single large eye in the middle of his head. As I looked at this alien's eye, it felt as though it penetrated my chest and my right lung. In my mind, I thought that it might have been looking at something in my chest or removing something that was there. I don't know what happened with this vision, but it was the first time I felt something physical with a vision.

It is important for me to discuss my thought disorders and delusions related to people with tattoos. I believed people with tattoos were aliens. People get tattoos mostly on their legs or arms, but some get them on their backs and faces as well. A lot of people with tattoos are very young, and I started to believe there was something very different about these people. I couldn't understand how parents allowed their children to get tattoos, as I would never allow my children to get them.

I started to believe that people with tattoos were not from earth because of their age and the fact that these tattoos looked like they had been on their arms for a long time. I sometimes felt like I missed things over the years.

CHAPTER 16

DEALING WITH ALL THE THOUGHTS AND DELUSIONS

In 2013, I spent the whole year battling the thought disorders and delusions that came from the previous years. I waited for January 11 to come around so I could possibly see another vision like the one that had happened in 2012. But when it came, nothing happened. I was disappointed because I had been anticipating something would happen. Later in the spring, I realized that the alcohol I had consumed over the years had different effects on my mood and mind.

Alcohol is a depressant, and drinking a lot of it can affect a person's mood. With me, delusions were always present, but I also found I had different thoughts depending on what alcohol I drank; even the manufacturer of the alcohol affected my thoughts. For example, over the years, beer such as Coors Light or Michelob Ultra would keep my mood steady during the night. If I decided to drink a beer such as Sam Adams or Heineken, my mood would change a little—it would go from steady to upset and mean in nature. The same would happen when I drank hard liquor such as whiskey, while drinking wine kept me steady as well. I began to only drink certain spirits, and with the amount of medication I was taking for my mental illness, I never got drunk. Over the years, I mostly drank at home by myself. It was safe knowing I did not have to worry about getting pulled over for driving under the influence of alcohol. I also spent a lot of time at home, just so I wouldn't have to go out and deal with other people and the thought disorders and delusions that would be brought about by being in a bar.

The last vacation we took as a family happened in the spring 2013, when we went to the Mall of America in Minnesota. This was a trip like all the others – my delusions did not stop. We stayed in a hotel that was relatively close to the mall and was connected to the mall and downtown by a train. Because it was a train, like a subway, my mind started in on the delusion that a new rail line was going to appear because of my causing it to appear. We took the train to the largest mall and spent the day there.

We spent time in the Microsoft store, which had an electronic table. You could push the numbers on the table, and it acted like a calculator. I manipulated this in my mind to think that I was pushing certain numbers and somehow writing computer code again, remembering the delusion I'd had in Chicago. I also envisioned the table electronics rising up to have a three-dimensional view.

We ate at Dick's Last Resort restaurant, and I missed out on a lot of the fun because of my delusions. When we got back to the hotel, things were better in my mind, and the next morning, my mind was somewhat normal.

We walked around stores and buildings in Minneapolis. We stopped at a coin shop in one of the buildings to purchase an old coin. We walked through the Wells Fargo building and saw the old horse carriage. And we went up to the observation deck of one of the old buildings and looked over the city of Minneapolis. All the while, I continued to believe others were listening to my thoughts. Though nothing unusual happened, as we headed back to Topeka, as with previous trips, I was relieved we were heading home.

I had an interesting experience going to the eye doctor. My eyes were normal, despite the small round dot in my left eye. I was having a delusional experience when I was having the eye exam. The exam involved covering the left eye and reading the words on the chart and then covering the right eye and reading the words on the chart. I don't know if this is normal, and I never asked the doctor, but when I would switch eyes, I would see a completely new set of letters. I suppose this is normal so you don't try to fake it and say the same words for each eye, but I thought something different. I thought the chart was the same for both eyes, and for some unexplained reason, I was seeing two different letter charts; therefore, one eye was different from the other. I would think of the times when I had experienced the left and right sides and believed this had something to do with the different charts.

In the hallway of my bedroom, I found mysterious marks in the carpet. I have three cats, but they couldn't have made these marks. When I rubbed the marks out and vacuumed them, they were gone for a day, but then they showed back up. I believed there was some kind of spell that was put there for a reason unknown to me. In addition, I also thought there was a creature making its way from the main bathroom through the hall and into the bedroom every night. Fortunately, I was not scared of any of the visions or delusions. If I was scared, I would be afraid to fall asleep at night, fearing a creature was in my bedroom.

There had been times when I was in a hypomania mood, and I would have to do something such as checking in to see my nurse practitioner or purchasing an item. In cases such as these, someone would ask me to sign my name on a receipt. I thought at the time the purpose of asking me to sign my name was so they could tell whether I was off in my mood and mind. But I was paranoid to sign my name, thinking they were going to use it for something else. I later understood that, in situations such as this, in which someone is suffering from mental illness, asking for a signature is an extra step that would determine how someone's mind was acting. Sometimes they would use the word "autograph" and that would, in some cases, set me into a thought disorder. This was something that, with time, would slowly disappear.

I have laid out how I saw and heard things over the years, but I have not yet touched on the correlation between thinking something and another person making a sound. For example, let's say I was at the grocery store, and I would think of an item I needed to purchase; someone would drop something, and it would make a loud noise, or someone would sneeze. I would believe these actions were tied to my thoughts, as I continued to believe others could hear my thoughts. I would sometimes wonder if the actions—like sneezing—were in response to something I remembered, like an item of food. I would have a sensitivity toward people's facial expressions or words. I just amplified those emotions and senses to include common everyday things that happen with people.

Donating clothes to Good Will is not a big deal, but for me, one incident had me believing I was in hell. I was dropping off a bag of children's clothes one day and noticed the man who took my bags had red eyes. I started to think he was a demon and I was in hell. He was nice and didn't do anything that would be considered mean, but I couldn't look him straight in the eyes. I never met anyone else around Topeka with red eyes. I thought about that delusion for the rest of the day.

The final vision I had in 2013 was of a split screen, just like some of my other visions were. A person dressed as a robot was in my view to the right. The person looked like an alien bounty hunter. He wore a helmet on his head, and it covered up his face. On the left side of my vision was a creature that looked like a cross between a human and an animal; the creature was black in color, and its tongue was sticking out. I could not make heads or tails of what that two-sided vision was about. One side looked to be from the future, and the other the past.

When I looked in the mirror at my reflection, I would wonder if I was seeing myself or someone else. Could there be a simple explanation for why I was thinking these thoughts? People take for granted that they are looking at themselves in the mirror, but not me. I couldn't help but wonder if that was my reflection or if it was someone else's seeing me.

I used to take trips to Kansas City with my son and daughter. I would take one or the other and spend several hours going to the mall or just driving around. My mind was so messed up on so many of those trips. With the radio going and things entering my mind, it was a struggle to make sure they were having fun. The mall in Kansas City created uncomfortable situations wherein I had to keep my anxiety from rising because of all the people walking around. My thoughts would start going, and it would not get any better until we left the mall.

On several occasions, I would unnecessarily get upset with my daughter because she would always forget to bring her phone charger on our trips. We would always have to stop at a store and buy a new one. What made me upset was not her, but the fact that this happened more than once. It was like I was going around in circles in my head, and this event repeated itself. I tried not to think too much about it, but I would be reminded that it had taken place before, whether it was having to buy a phone charger or driving to a location.

I have touched on issues related to my thought disorders, but I want to talk in depth about the struggles I had with my mind and the belief that everyone could hear what I was thinking. Of all the visions and delusions I had over the years, none of them were worse than believing others could hear what I was thinking. For someone without a mental illness, thoughts like these would never come up. But the notion that my thoughts were overheard drove me deeper and deeper into paranoia. Just think about how you would feel if you thought these thoughts. It is difficult for someone without a mental illness to imagine this thought disorder. I spent years battling this thought, and everyone I would meet would be a part of this thinking. I spent years trying, to no avail, to compartmentalize my thoughts and control them. How could I control something that continually entered my mind?

In addition, associations were a major part of my delusions. These thoughts were very strong in the earlier years. I had to learn to let go of trying to control them and, instead, try to redirect my mind onto something else.

I would try to concentrate on something I had to get done or some television show or movie to redirect my thinking, but watching television and talking with people was extremely difficult. I cannot recall a single face-to-face conversation I had with someone that did not leave me paranoid. Over the years, it would drive me into a situation where I spent as little time as possible in the City of Topeka and spent a lot more time at home working on projects around the house. This isolation helped me overall, with the thoughts eventually disappearing completely.

I ultimately cut off all communication with my friends from high school. In the past, whenever we would get together, the opportunity for my mind to start thinking about their words and whether they were hearing what I was thinking emerged. It was not fun at all to be around friends and have this happen. My lack of interaction with people did not have a negative impact on my mind; if I had to choose between being with my friends and dealing with thought disorders or working around the house, I would choose to be alone.

I was not entirely isolated; my son would come home from college, and I would spend some time with my daughter. During the week, I would get my coffee in the morning and purchase a paper for my father. I would then spend forty-five minutes talking to my father. I had a mental illness, but I could manage it around them.

CHAPTER 17

TIME WARP

With regards to time, I always felt time went by more slowly than normal—and it was somehow only slower for me. How could this be possible? I always felt I was left behind and always behind everyone else.

If I went through a drive-through, I believed the people in front of me were just a little faster in getting there. I even started to believe they were getting their food for free. There were many times that I would be behind someone, and in a split second, they would be driving off with their food.

One time, in the bathroom at my house, I noticed a piece of paper with a folded edge sitting on the counter. When I looked at it, the edge moved slightly and continued to do so every time I looked at it. I thought I was in a time warp or a loop and wondered if this was possible. Could there be different time lines with multiple things going on? If it was eight in the morning, could there be something else happening at nine in the morning or even three in the afternoon?

I started to think about daylight saving time and wondered whether someone living on the East Coast could possibly know what was going to happen in the middle of the country or the West Coast.

To emphasize this delusional thought, I thought back to the time I bid on one of the phases at the wastewater treatment plant and received several prices for the equipment needed for the project. One of the prices was from a company on the East Coast, and the other was from a company on the West Coast. Close to bidding time, the company from the East Coast cut its price by several thousand dollars, making its bid lower than that of the West Coast company. I somehow managed to convince myself to believe the East Coast company knew what its competitor on the West Coast was going to bid. My mind was just messing with me.

While I was driving down the road, a car would sometimes drive more slowly in front of me, and if I needed to turn in a certain direction, it would do the same. It was as though I was being followed, but I was doing the following. Later, I would be less anxious and would stop thinking these things.

At other times, I would be driving and a song would come on, and I'd talk to myself. What was strange was that I'd believed I'd already done that before, sometimes even saying the exact same thing.

One time during a golf tournament, it felt like time accelerated, and we should have been on the fourteenth hole rather than the fourth. It's hard to describe, but I felt as though I was behind. When we finally got to the fourteenth hole, all the golfers were backed up. When we finished our round, it felt as though we were ahead one day.

At this time, a vision would always exaggerate my delusional thinking. A specific vision that would exaggerate my delusions was a series of windows floating and turning around in space. The windows had different pictures on them, but I could not make out what they were.

One time I was sitting on the couch in the living room when my stomach started to feel upset. I had experienced the same feeling when I was admitted to Stormont Vail West. My body felt weightless, while at the same time I felt as though I experienced an earthquake without the house and floors shaking. The next day, I heard there had been an earthquake in Oklahoma. I wondered, Could I have felt this from hundreds of miles away? In this instance, I was able to redirect my thinking and not give into this delusion.

Another example of things that annoyed me around the house was keeping the cat's water bowl full. I would fill the bowl up, and the next day it would be empty. I even went out and bought a larger bowl so that it would last longer, but it did not change anything. It always seemed to be at the same level. This still happens, but it no longer annoys me.

When my son graduated from high school, we threw him a graduation party at the house. A couple of his friends attended along with other people. During this party, I had an episode. It started when I left the house to pick up food for the event. I had this strange feeling my family was trying to get me out of the house. I thought that maybe, by the time I would come back, the party would have happened and ended.

At the end of the party, one of the guests mentioned getting a gin and tonic. I thought it was an odd comment to make and wondered whether he was trying to get my mind going. I thought about the words, letters, and numbers associated with gin and tonic. After thinking of the words and letters, I did not pursue this anymore.

CHAPTER 18

THE YEAR OF THE VISIONS

I had more visions and thought disorders in 2014 than I had in any of the previous years. The first vision I had was in the early part of the year. I was sitting on a chair in the house with my eyes closed, and I saw a man's head with a planet in front of him. The planet moved from right to left in my view and disappeared in the man's right eye, which is my left side. In comparison to the planet, the man's head was enormous. After seeing this, I then saw, on my right side, a giant red person falling to the ground.

The next vision I had looked like it came straight out of the movies. Again, I was sitting in a chair at my house. This time, I saw a picture of a half man, half robot. The robotic person was facing me. On the right was the man, in the middle was a line, and on the left was the red robot eye. I immediately thought back to years ago when my illness started and I had seen other pairs of red eyes, starting with those of the woman on television.

On March 16, 2014, I had one of two visions within that month. In the evening on this day, I was watching a television show that started at 9:30 p.m. It was only minutes into the show when the actors did something funny, and I started to laugh. I laughed so hard that I couldn't catch my breath. I tilted my head back on the chair without getting any air, and with my eyes closed, I saw some lights going on in my head, as if I'd just had a stroke.

When I opened my eyes again, the television acted like it had just turned on again and it had been off when this was taking place. I was not positive that I had a stroke, but it might have happened. After opening my eyes, I got the strangest feeling that someone had just arrived or left from my mind. It was an out-of-body experience, and even though everything was the same in the living room, something definitely took place.

On March 20, I was not feeling well mentally, so I took a short nap at home. When I was trying to fall asleep, another vision happened. It was a picture of a creature that looked like a lizard with a tail. The way I saw it made it look like it was inside my stomach. In the vision, the lizard disappeared like a time-lapse video. Was this thing causing me to have delusions and thought disorders? I thought back to before I had been admitted to Stormont West and how my mind and my stomach had been out of control.

After this vision, I believed I was getting closer to an answer. I believed something would happen, and I would no longer have these thought disorders, visions, or delusions. I believed it was only a few more months away. This vision and the event that took place on March 16 changed my thoughts about working at the construction company.

September 13 came around, and this time there was another vision. This vision was of an angel floating above a dark place, and from below, pairs of blue eyes started to appear. Once they appeared, the many eyes moved from the bottom of my vision to the top of my vision. I thought these people had probably been around for a long time, and they might have been going to heaven. I was reminded of my mother's, father's, and grandmother's blue eyes.

I tried to associate blue with everything, from Blue Valley School District in Kansas City to Ford Motor Company. My mind could not leave out the color of the sky and the color of the oceans. I thought maybe these people had to go through the same thing I was going through. Did they make it through, or did they fail?

I also thought that the number 14 might have had something to do with keeping those people in the same place for many years. If these people were the number 13, then did that mean they were before 14, since 13 is before 14? I then started to think about the letter and number associations and how the letter *A* is the number 1 and how this could be related to blue. The month of May has the letter *M*, which is 13 and *a*, which is 1. The word "Nazi" had the letter *N*, which is 14 and the letter *a*, which is 1. Was the *Na* before or after the letters *Ma*?

During fall 2014, I had a disturbing vision of three men walking toward me like they were zombies. The man in the middle was just like a zombie from the movies.

This vision was in color, so I saw the full magnitude of it. I started to wonder if a zombie apocalypse was going to take place in the future, just like many shows movies portrayed. Fortunately, it would not be long until my next vision, so my mind worked that thought for a short period.

On November 20, 2014, I had a feeling while seeing my nurse practitioner at a different mental health facility. Standing in line behind me at the front desk was a health professional and patient. As I listened to their conversation, it felt as though I was answering the professional's questions. I associated this with the vision I'd had on March 20, 2014. The two dates were eight months apart, and I began to wonder whether it was possible if eight years could represent eight months. I was computing 11s, 10s, 8s, 6s, and many other numbers. There was even the number 1 in my mind, representing one year, one month, or one week. These thoughts would do plenty to my state of mind.

On November 28, I saw a vision of a man's head again. The head appeared in front of me and then looked right and left and then went straight up out of my view. When the head went straight up, it turned from a living head into a skull. After the skull disappeared, I saw another man's head but this one came from the right of my view and exited to the far left and did not change into a skull. Was the first man someone from Nazi Germany? I got nowhere again with my question. A couple of days later, on November 30, I saw another vision.

Initially, I did not see anything but heard someone say, "Thank you for protecting my son." After the voice, a person appeared that resembled Jesus. The person then transformed into a butterfly and flew away. I thought to myself, *Was that Jesus?* Was I ultimately going through all of this to protect him? I then thought of the vision of the man going down the escalator and thought maybe that was who that was. You can imagine how my mind started to run and think of all sorts of different things. Was the voice I'd heard the voice of God? How in the world could I be involved in something so major?

I remember thinking over the years that if I was involved in something as big as this, then I could not do anything more in my life that would ever be a greater calling. Being successful in business or in life is a wonderful thing, but to have helped Jesus would be the greatest. In mid-December 2014, I saw my last two visions of the year.

They occurred one after the other on December 14. The first vision was a man who had a crocodile head, and the second vision was of a man who looked like electricity was coming out of the top and sides of his head. These two images did not scare me but made me quickly open my eyes. In my mind, I was trying to put a name on those two visions, relating this to the same day that I saw those two demons in 2004. The relation between these visions and the previous vision only had the day in common. I thought there also had to be something related to Nero or the Nazis because of the letter and number 14.

CHAPTER 19

2015 AND THE NUMBER 26

The start of the year was the same as the previous years, with confusion, questions, and no answers. On February 26, I was resting in the chair in a side room of the house when a vision occurred. This vision was of a person who looked like me. It emerged from my right side and then appeared in the center. It was a floating head. The head laughed, and then the eye started to change and get older. The head then came straight at me and turned into a skull. The face looked like me and I started to wonder whether it represented the number 26—because of the day. I was born on the twenty-seventh, so was this person in front of me all these years? I couldn't get this thought out of my head. If this was possible, then this person might have been causing all my problems. I tried to come up with another number sequence; this time, it was the year 2015 and the number 26, with the difference between 26 and 15 being 11 or K in the alphabet. The number 11 was significant to me because of the month of February. In the word "February" the letters F and e represented the numbers 6 and 5, or 11 if added together.

Later, in early summer, I would see what I thought was Nero laying on his side with what looked like many flies swarming his body. I could not tell if he was just sleeping or if he was dead, but I think he was dead. The flies could have been the insects, but in my mind, I thought back to when I had seen ghosts flying around; this made me think that maybe the flies were ghosts flying around him. I thought it was Nero because his name starts with an N, and per the internet, he committed suicide in AD 68, with the 6 and 8 equaling 14. I was born in 1968, so was I connected to him because of these dates? It drove me crazy to be thinking that there was a relation between AD 68 and AD 1968. The obvious was the difference in the numbers—1900. Did the difference of 1900 represent the twentieth century, or was it only a number? I kept working this, trying to find a piece that would make sense.

This year was also the year that I saw a woman in one of my visions. I saw a picture of a man holding onto a woman. His arms were wrapped around her, and the woman looking off in a daze. Normally, that would not be a big deal, but in this case, the woman had long hair and bright blue eyes. Her eyes were very bright blue, as though a light was shining behind them, and they resembled the eyes I had seen in the blue-eyed people in a previous vision. In my mind, I felt like that vision had something to do with rescuing that woman.

In the fall, I had a vision of Germany again, but this time of World War I. I saw a black-and-white picture of the Kaiser of Germany in front of older soldiers. I could only think that these soldiers were of the general rank because of their uniforms. After I saw that vision, another vision appeared—a box with six war medals. The medals had edging around them to make them look like the rays of the sun or the triangles you draw to indicate petals around a flower. I call the man Kaiser because he had a horned helmet like Kaiser Wilhelm wore during World War I. I tried to piece together what relation there was between World War I and World War II, but I never found any relation.

In mid-December, I had my last vision of the year. It happened on December 16. It was a split screen with a line down the middle. On the left side of my view was a tall man with dark brown hair. I could only see up from his chest, and the man did not move in my view. On the right side of my view was a man's head facing the man on the left. The man's head kissed the centerline between the two views and then moved up and disappeared. All I could make out about this man was that he had a mustache and could have been Hitler. I thought perhaps the man on the right was happy about the man on the left. I could only think that the man on the left was some religious person, such as a saint or someone. Maybe that was the goal of all the visions and delusions over the years, along with Jesus. When I didn't have references or answers to anything, I would come up with all types of scenarios. At least this vision was related to heaven and not pictures of people with sharp teeth or aliens.

CHAPTER 20

THE FLYING WITCH AND THE CATS

It wasn't until the start of 2016 that I noticed something strange when I closed my eyes. At first, it just looked like a black dot moving around, but later that year, it got close enough for me to get a good look at it. It was a man with a black pointy witch's hat, sitting on a broom. He would fly around, disappear, and then reappear again. This sounds crazy, but I was confident in what I was seeing, and it wouldn't be until February 23, 2017, that I saw a good close-up of the man as he disappeared. In 2016 and the beginning of 2017, I wondered who this person might be. When I saw a close-up of him on February 23, I started to believe the man represented the number 23. I also thought it was strange that, after I'd had this vision, one of my cats would come into my room and start meowing. Could my cat be the number 23? I also thought that maybe the man flew around in my eye, making sure I'd see certain things and blocking others out.

During this time, I also spent one night in the cloud manipulation delusion. It happened to be a stormy night with a possibility of a tornado happening. I would see a low-hanging cloud in a group of clouds, and I would try to control its movement so it would not go toward the ground and start a tornado. This delusion didn't last long, and I stopped thinking of this delusion within hours.

On August 21, I saw something that could help explain the problems I'd had during this time. It was a picture of me around ten years old, and I could see a part of my body and my face. There were tubes attached to my head, as though I was wired into something. Could I be asleep somewhere with these things attached to my mind? Could all my thoughts and delusions have been created by something that was not me? If this was something that could happen in the future, then how did my age in that vision fit into this scenario?

The strangest thing I saw this year did not come in a vision; it was a lingerie commercial on television. At the end of the commercial, one of the models walked to the center of the screen and stuck her tongue out. I could have sworn her tongue was six inches long—like that of a demon. I wondered if I was the only one who saw that tongue.

Over the past three years, I made many new improvements to my house. I completed many outdoor projects, ranging from landscaping to a fire pit area, which made the entire house look better. I think completing all those projects over the years was like therapy. I had to plan what I wanted to do and then come up with the materials and get it built. It was such a relief to me that, over the last three years, the projects got more complex. But my mind was getting better, so they were not too complex for me to build. In the beginning of my mental illness, and for many years thereafter, I would not even think about doing home improvements, as I wasn't capable mentally or physically to perform the work. If a project would have come to mind during that time, my mind would not have allowed me to do it.

My son stays with me sometimes, but he's off at college, and so I live by myself. Therefore, I have three cats in the house, Rocky, Cinnamon, and Sammy, to keep me company. I got Rocky and Cinnamon from the local humane shelter around eleven years ago. Sammy was an early Christmas present that showed up on the deck outside the house on Christmas Eve in 2009, so he is several years younger than Rocky and Cinnamon.

During the years of my mental illness, I developed another delusion. Depending on the situation—which usually involved me leaving the house or going out to the garage and back inside—the cats always fixated on my shoes. In the beginning, I did not think anything of it, but as the years went by, I started to wonder why they were looking at my shoes. I believed they were seeing different shoes or people at different times of the day. Sometimes Sammy would be at the door, and sometimes it would be Rocky or Cinnamon. Sometimes Sammy would run away in fright, and sometimes Rocky and Cinnamon would do the same.

Another interesting point I want to talk about involves my shoes. Randomly, or so it seemed, my shoelaces—either the left or the right—would come undone.

This might not seem like a big deal to someone, but sometimes they would seem to untie themselves, just by my looking at them.

I also believed my cats could read minds. I would be petting Cinnamon in one room, and Rocky or Sammy would show up. This is probably normal in all cats, but do all cats try to sit to the back left, the back right, or exactly behind you?

Sometimes when I would eat something or go to the restroom, sure enough, one of them was eating and going to the restroom. It was just the strangest thing. I eventually started associating the three cats with people; I'd imagine they were little people walking around.

When the cats would rub my leg, I would think they were trying to pick up a spirit or ghost. The cats would even try to lick my spoon or bowl after I finished eating, which is normal. But in my mind, I thought they were trying to get into my head somehow. Sometimes, I would notice the cats trying to stare at me like they were trying to hypnotize me. Over the years, they would even have a meow that began to annoy me, and I would start to believe they were trying to connect to something.

The cats in the house would not only sit on the left or right or behind me, they would also cross in front, under my legs, moving from one side to the other. I would say there were times that it annoyed me, so I would put my feet down to stop them from running. Something in my delusional mind was telling me that there was more to this action than just running from one side to the other. I guess you could say I was as crazy as a cat myself for these thoughts.

CHAPTER 21

THE MOBILE PHONE
PEOPLE ARE IN MY HEAD

Over the years, I had developed some delusions centered around others telling me to look at things—whether they be on a computer, a mobile phone, a television, or things around the house. I would get irritated at the news and the weather forecast because the anchors and weathermen always wanted me to look at something. I thought their requests went deeper than just "looking at something." I believed that, by complying and looking at what they wanted me to look at, I would enable them to get into my head and somehow use my eyes. That sounds crazy, but there have been many occasions where I would think something strange was happening.

Whenever I talked to someone and the person would interrupt what I was saying, did that mean he or she had the power to change things? An example of this was when I had the air units in my house serviced because of issues with the temperature. The repairman was in the basement and asked me to come down to the utility room. When I got there, he told me the coil in the unit was frozen. When I looked at it, I saw that it was indeed completely frozen, but for some reason, I thought that the coil was not frozen. When he said, "See, the coil is frozen," and I looked at the coil, I believed I had managed to freeze it—given that, by this time, I knew my eyes could change things so rapidly I wouldn't even notice. This of course was also related to my discussions regarding time and how I believed it moved more slowly for me than it did for anyone else. This was an example of how things could be manipulated.

I talked earlier about my difficulties with believing people heard what I was thinking, but I have not yet touched on another delusional disorder I was having during those years. It involved people and how I interpreted their conversations and the way they acted toward each other. Specifically, I believed I was the only one who could not connect on the level others could—that they were able to communicate among themselves just by looking into each other's eyes. I associated this with telepathy seen in movies. So, not only could other people hear my thoughts, they were also talking among themselves, and I was clueless as to what was being discussed.

I talked a little about how my eyes would move to pick up words and try to put them together. I was doing the same thing with people, reading their postures or tones of voice. Later, I would notice how people would walk by each other and give a little head nod. It was not very noticeable, but I picked up on it, and it set me off into believing others were telepathic. Maybe in the future, as people evolve, they might have that gift. But in the present, it was not possible. These thoughts only isolated me even more from the rest of the world. I believed that maybe I had the same gift, but in my case, it evolved into a nightmare in my mind and paranoia about others hearing my thoughts. What connection was there in looking others straight in the eyes? Later, I was finally able to stop myself from these delusions.

Sometimes, when I would go to the hardware store to pick up some supplies for a project I was working on at home, I'd find people in the same area of the store that I was in. This happened all the time. They would be standing next to me when I was trying to find a screw length or size, for example, and I would get confused and forget what I was looking for. I started to believe the people had something to do with my confusion. Somehow, they could interrupt my thought process, and I'd end up purchasing the wrong item. I did not realize I had the wrong item until I was back at home trying to work on the project. I would then have to go back to the store and get the correct item. This could have been a result of my anxiety or having been thrown off by listening in on people's conversations as I was choosing my items. Nowadays, when I go to the hardware store and someone is standing next to me, it does not bother me, and I know he or she is not getting inside my head. I still occasionally purchase the wrong item for the job, but it's never because of my delusions.

I had another vision of a bald man on a mobile telephone walking toward me.

Prior to this, I was always suspicious of people with mobile phones. I always noticed people walking around with a phone to their ear. That's no big thing, right? To me, it appeared as though people with a mobile phone attached to their ear would just show up in certain places around Topeka. I started to believe people with phones could somehow travel around to different places in the city, or elsewhere, just by using their mobile phones.

Somehow I would tie this information to the cloud over the earth. Even storage for computers was called "the cloud." I started to notice that the cell towers in Topeka were roughly the same height as the deck on my house. Could Topeka be the highest city in the world? Could Topeka be in the clouds? Could it be a place that was not real but only an illusion generated by computers or machines? In my mind, it was a possibility, but there was no proof. Was this happening because of the invention of the smart phone? Could the switch from analog to digital phones have anything to do with this?

Computers, phones, and software have been rapidly expanding, with new technology coming out every year. I would sometimes wonder whether the world had aged hundreds or even thousands of years and wondered whether I could have completely missed these years. Could the mobile phone be a transportation device for humans or aliens?

Chapter 22

The Last Year, 2017

Over the past ten months, I'd noticed something taking place only when I was trying to fall asleep. This had occurred on and off for years, but I didn't realize it until 2017. Occasionally, if I did not have a vision, it felt like my body was ramped up on energy, and I could not fall asleep. On some occasions, I would lie in bed for over an hour until it finally felt like some energy was discharged from my body, and I was powering down for the night. Once this took place, I could fall asleep easily.

Later in the spring, I had a vision while asleep in a chair. This vision was like the vision I'd had in 2012 with my left eye and someone else's right eye disconnecting. This time, there was a bright white light when the eyes disconnected. I could see an outline of someone's head but could not identify who it was.

Lately, my visions had been occurring in the afternoon around two o'clock. During these times, I would see a picture of a human skull, but the brain cavity was bigger in size than a normal human head. I would try to associate it with a movie or television show I watched.

Another time during this year when I was mowing the lawn, I looked over at a car driving by and thought I saw a dog's head on a human's body driving the car. I thought about this for a couple of hours while I mowed the lawn, but it eventually left my mind. At this point, it was easier to not think of delusions.

I had a couple of visions between August 5, 2017, and August 12, 2017. The Topeka West thirty-year class reunion was taking place on August 5, but despite repeated phone calls from my high school girlfriend and some friends, I did not attend the reunion. Nor did I respond to my friends or high school girlfriend. Even though my mind was now somewhat in control of things, I figured it would not be wise to attend the reunion. I don't believe I would have had the same issues I'd had at my twenty-year reunion, but I wanted to steer clear just in case.

In the afternoon of August 5, at around four o'clock, I was sitting in a chair at my house and saw several things. The first thing I saw was an old pale man who looked like he was one of the Romans. Next, there was a side view of a person who had very hypnotizing eyes and a missing tooth. In this vision, the face focused on the left side of my view. After that vision disappeared, a woman on her hands and knees with brilliant blue eyes and long hair emerged. Her eyes were the same color blue as the woman I wrote about earlier. It was the first thing I focused on. After the woman, I saw an overweight man walking around the left side of my view, but he looked normal.

Later in the week, I sat in the opposite chair in the study and saw several more people. A bright light emerged when I closed my eyes, and I saw a man's face floating off from a circular spotlight perspective in my vision. It almost felt as though the man and I were connected through our eyes before he broke off and floated away. A couple of seconds later, I saw someone completely in red, and as my view inside the hole got closer, I was able to see the person's eyes were also red.

Other things, such as someone putting his or her hand on my shoulder or grazing someone's hand when exchanging money, would put me into a thought disorder state. I would start to wonder why people were touching me and whether they were intentionally trying to make me feel uncomfortable. The same could be said about people who are close talkers. They would always make me feel so uncomfortable. I would also never make eye contact with someone I was talking to. I would get anxiety just by looking into a person's eyes.

I have a mild case of obsessive-compulsive disorder. Things always had to be in a certain order; if they were not, I would get upset. When the house got cleaned, I would have to go around and put things back the way I wanted them to be. This used to be an area of annoyance I had to deal with along with all the delusions and thought disorders, but I am now at the point where it does not bother me. In the past, compartmentalizing helped me with my bipolar disorder. On the other hand, I never had a fear of getting dirty. I know some people have issues with being clean all the time, so I was fortunate to be spared this disorder. I only had some mental illnesses; not all of them. But the mental illnesses I had were monumentally challenging.

There are still moments in my life that I find annoying. For example, when I would go to the library to write this book, someone would come and sit right next to me, despite the room being full of empty chairs.

I sometimes think that I am just making my way through space and time—that I have not arrived at my destination yet, whether it be here or somewhere else at some other time. Maybe all these visions I had were timed exactly to when I was supposed to see them. If I am still making my way, then someday I might reach my destination and be fully aware of the past twelve years of my life. With all the things that I have gone through over these years, my only wish would be to know if there is any truth behind my delusions. I believe there is some type of truth that is to come for me. I would not have all those visions without having some explanation of who or what they were. I do a good job of blocking out the thought disorders and delusions now. I think I have had a little victory in that area.

Throughout these past twelve years, as well as my entire life, I have always tried to be honest. I believe being honest has helped with my mental illness over the years. It has helped keep me on a moral and ethical course. Furthermore, if there were times when I would not know something—which were plenty—I would not talk about it, for fear of being incorrect. There is a part of me that strives to be as accurate as possible in my conversations with others, sometimes rendering me completely silent. I have always had a good heart and been considerate of other people's feelings, but these past twelve years certainly put my emotions in chaos.

CHAPTER 23

TWELVE YEARS OF MEDICATION

I went through a lot of medication over the years to find the right one for my bipolar disorder. I first started taking Depakote and Effexor, and later started taking Geodon with these. I took the Depakote and Effexor when I was admitted at Stormont Vail West. The Geodon was added later in the year. I took this medication for the rest of 2005 into 2006, but it did not work well for me. It clouded my head, and I still had delusions. I would always take my medication nightly, around eight thirty, and would turn the pill containers upside down to remind me I had taken it.

By the middle of 2006, I had switched to a different bipolar medication. I started to get a side effect from the Geodon I was taking. The side effect was tardive dyskinesia, which causes an uncontrollable shaking of either the legs or arms. If this happens while taking the medication, it is advised to get off the medication right away, as the shaking could potentially become permanent. In my case, my right arm would shake violently while I brushed my teeth at night. I had to use my left hand to stop the shaking of the right.

The next medication I started taking was Lamictal. After taking the Lamictal for several months, I started to have a side effect associated with this medication as well. Rashes started to appear on the skin around my face. They were large enough in size for people to notice, and the moisturizer I was using did not help.

Later, I started taking lithium in small doses and then gradually increased the doses. Of all the medications I took over the years, this medication put me in the most horrible state of depression. The thoughts I was having were still present; my severe depression only slowed them down. This medication did not work for me either, so I only took it for a couple of months.

To counter the depression I was experiencing, I started taking an antidepressant medication called Wellbutrin. By taking this medication, I noticed a difference in my overall mood—I experienced the same racing thoughts as I had before my first mental breakdown. After talking with the nurse, I steered clear of that type of medication and any other medication in the same class.

Lithium did not cause any side effects, but it definitely made me look and feel like I wasn't on this planet. While taking all these medications, my delusions never stopped, and they continued to drive me crazy. In 2007, after I got off the lithium, I was prescribed Zyprexa. This medication is normally used for schizophrenia but can also be used to treat bipolar disorder. I took this medication for several months, but I still did not feel good.

After Zyprexa, I was prescribed Seroquel XR in 2007. The "XR" in the name meant it was an extended release medication. It helped clear my head and pulled me out of my depression. I took this medication until 2017. I started at a low dose and then eventually increased the medication to 1,200 mg, taking three 400 mg tablets nightly. If there was ever a day that my mind was totally out of control, I would take the Seroquel, along with a small dose of Zyprexa to add an extra boost to the Seroquel. This combination helped me sleep at night.

Over the years, I might have forgotten to take my medicine a total of ten times. I would always know by lunchtime the next day if I had forgotten to take it the night before, because I would get up around five or five thirty and have a lot of energy to start the day. As the morning went by, I would start to sweat, and my mind would start to race. By noon, I would have to make a trip back to the house and take another dose. In the beginning, it was like taking one to one and a half doses because I would take it again at bedtime, but it did not make me feel more medicated.

There were no limits to some of the delusions and thoughts I had. I even tried to make a connection between AstraZeneca, the manufacturer of Seroquel and myself. "Astra" means stars, and the seal of Kansas has this word. Could there be a connection? I thought. Since the company is from England, I wondered whether there was a connection between Kansas and England. I thought about this for months.

I want to talk about the costs of some of these medications. Unfortunately, there are people with mental illness who cannot afford some of these medications. As far as the costs go, lithium is the cheapest of the medications, as it has been around for a long time and is a generic drug. For many years, this was one of the main medications used to treat the mentally ill. I had the luxury to be able to take many medications in the search for the right one. I did not have to think about the price. But for others, lithium was and is the only option.

The prices for the medications I took varied from a few dollars to thousands of dollars. Taking Seroquel for ten years was very expensive. This medication cost approximately $2 a milligram. I started at a low dose, but once I was up to 1,200 mg, the price went up to $2,400. My medication was covered under insurance, so I only had to pay less than $100. Can you imagine having to pay $28,800 per year for this medication out of pocket? People who work at jobs that pay $10 per hour for forty hours a week, four weeks a month for twelve months, earn less than $20,000 per year.

I am a larger person in height and weight, so my dose was always higher. Additionally, the doses I was given were also in relation to my mental issues. On the other hand, smaller people might only be prescribed 150 milligrams, for example. Regardless, that still adds up to $300 per month, which is a significant amount of money for people who earn minimum wage and don't have health insurance. Hopefully, costs of these medications will drop so people can decide which medication works best for them.

Some medications are made by generic companies, and I picked up my first generic medication last month and have been taking it for several weeks now with the same effect as the name brand version. I might make an adjustment to the 1,200 mg I am taking, depending on whether I lose weight.

Weight gain is a side effect of some mental disorder medications. I gained a significant amount of weight over the years but eventually lost a lot of the weight. I still have plenty of weight to lose to get to a place where I feel fit and healthy.

For the first couple of years, I went to see a therapist to discuss the thought disorders and delusions I was experiencing. I would meet with her once a month for an hour. I went through some hard times in the first several years, so it was good to talk to someone in the mental health field. I had talked to my wife about my problems, so my seeing a therapist also helped her. The appointments always started off the same, with the therapist asking how I was doing. I kept most of the thoughts I discussed in this book to myself and did not share these things with either the nurse or the therapist. I believed doing so would just complicate things for me in general. I don't know what would have happened had I discussed my issues with them during that time. I have no problems talking about them in this book because I am at the point where they don't bother me anymore. But back then, even when all of this was going on in my mind, I kept it locked in my mind. You could have talked to me during these years and never have known about the struggles I had been through. In the end, I stopped seeing the therapist but continued to see the nurse for medication and overall mental health–related issues.

CHAPTER 24

REACHING OUT TO PEOPLE WITH MENTAL ILLNESS

The goal of this book is to hopefully reach out to another person who may be suffering with bipolar disorder or any other mental illness. Reading this book may have helped you realize you might have experienced delusions of your own. The racing thoughts in a mental health patient with bipolar disorder are common in most people. There are other avenues for people suffering from mental illness. The National Association of Mental Illness (NAMI) has group meetings and other services that can help. During the twelve years of my struggle with mental illness, I never took advantage of NAMI's services, but they were offered to me. Some people might feel embarrassed to attend these meetings and talk about the issues they are having. I can understand that. For me, talking about my delusions and thought disorders in a group setting would have been difficult. Along with NAMI, there are books that you can read that may offer some additional help. The first step is to accept that you have a mental illness. I read in a NAMI letter that there are roughly sixty million people with some form of mental illness. There is still a stigma attached to having a mental illness, but medical advances and education have improved this.

My advice is to continue seeing a mental health professional whether it is a psychologist, nurse, or a therapist. It is important to keep seeing health care professionals so they can help you with your illness. They are trained in mental health and know of the medications that could possibly help with your condition. In my case, I saw a nurse practitioner throughout my twelve-year struggle. At first, the appointments were once a week, but after time, they decreased to monthly and then to every three months and, finally in 2017, to every six months.

I have been taking the same medication for many years now, and it has become part of my daily routine. It is important you keep taking your medications and let your health professional know if you are experiencing side effects like I did. For some people, it might never get much better, but don't give up. There might still be medications or other solutions, such as changing your routine, that can help you.

In this book, I did not mention things I did to help with my mental state. Some of the things I did included going to the gym and losing weight. This helped me both physically and mentally.

Having a mental illness is like being in a battle with your mind. This battle is not going to take a day or a week or a month, but might take years to win. Some people, like I did, might isolate themselves from others. If you are working and are uncomfortable interacting with others, then take time to ease yourself into situations. I used this technique when I was working, and although it did not make my delusions and thought disorders go away, it did make me feel better. I always felt accomplished after having a conversation with a coworker. I want to emphasize that I am not a mental health professional and only want to give you some advice to help you feel better. I wish you the best of luck and hope your mental illness improves.

ABOUT THE AUTHOR

Wolf Blaser Jr. travels to the darkest parts of his mind in this memoir about his battle with bipolar disorder.